YOUR QUESTIONS
GOD'S ANSWERS

Bible Answers to Some of Life's Most Challenging Issues

Family Home Christian Books

Printed by Remnant Publications

Printed in the United States of America

Cover design by David Berthiaume

Interior design by Nicole Warren

Images by Thinkstock.com unless otherwise noted

Project Contributors: Ken McFarland, Page One Communications;
Greg Solie • Altamont Graphics

ISBN: 978-1-5136-0030-7

CONTENTS

CHAPTER 1

By far, it is the world's best-selling book. Chances are, you have at least one copy of your own. Or perhaps you have heard many things about it but have never read it. Either way, you quite likely have questions about the Holy Bible—and fortunately, the Bible has all the answers about itself! So let us look at some of the most common questions people have about the Bible, and let it provide the answers.

Where did my Bible come from?

"All Scripture is given by inspiration of God." —2 Timothy 3:16.

"For prophecy never came by the will of man, but holy men of God spoke as they were moved by the Holy Spirit." —2 Peter 1:21.

"God, who at various times and in various ways spoke in time past to the fathers by the prophets." —Hebrews 1:1.

What is the purpose of the Bible?

"For whatever things were written before were written for our learning, that we through the patience and comfort of the Scriptures might have hope." —Romans 15:4.

"All Scripture … is profitable for doctrine, for reproof, for correction, for instruction in righteousness." —2 Timothy 3:16.

"That the man of God may be complete, thoroughly equipped for every good work." —2 Timothy 3:17.

"Your word is a lamp to my feet and a light to my path." —Psalm 119:105.

How can the Bible change me?

"Your word have I hidden in my heart, that I might not sin against You."—Psalm 119:11.

"How can a young man cleanse his way? By taking heed according to Your word." —Psalm 119:9.

"You are already clean because of the word which I have spoken to you." —John 15:3.

"By which have been given to us exceedingly great and precious promises, that through these you may be partakers of the divine nature, having escaped the corruption that is in the world through lust." —2 Peter 1:4.

"For this reason we also thank God without ceasing, because when you received the word of God which you heard from us, you welcomed it not as the word of men, but as it is in truth, the word of God, which also effectively works in you who believe." —1 Thessalonians 2:13.

"Having been born again, not of corruptible seed but incorruptible, through the word of God which lives and abides forever." —1 Peter 1:23.

"Sanctify them by Your truth. Your word is truth." —John 17:17.

The Divisions of Scripture

"Then He said to them, 'These are the words which I spoke to you while I was still with you, that all things must be fulfilled which were written in the *Law of Moses* and *the Prophets* and *the Psalms* concerning Me.'" —Luke 24:44, emphasis added.

NOTE: "The Law of Moses" refers to the first five books of the Old Testament. "The Prophets" included Isaiah, Jeremiah, Ezekiel, and the 12 minor prophets. "The Psalms" embraces all the remaining Old Testament books.

Why else is the Word so important?

IT IS ETERNAL:

"The grass withers, the flower fades, but the word of our God stands forever." —Isaiah 40:8.

AS OUR SPIRITUAL FOOD, IT IS MORE NECESSARY TO US THAN OUR PHYSICAL FOOD:

"I have not departed from the commandment of His lips; I have treasured the words of His mouth more than my necessary food." —Job 23:12.

GOD'S WORD IS POWERFUL:

"And they were astonished at His teaching, for His word was with authority." —Luke 4:32.

"What a word this is! For with authority and power He commands the unclean spirits, and they come out." —Luke 4:36.

The Two Great Questions We Should Ask as We Read God's Word

"You search the Scriptures, for in them you think you have eternal life; and these are they *which testify of Me.*" —John 5:39, emphasis added.

"And beginning at Moses and all the Prophets, He expounded to them in all the Scriptures the things concerning Himself." —Luke 24:27.

NOTE: When we open our Bible, our great desire should be to learn about Jesus—to come to know Him personally—to listen to Him speaking to us.

We can miss connecting one-on-one with Jesus if our primary purpose in reading the Word is to become theologically informed or to find texts here and there with which to defend our own points of view.

Bible facts and information are good to learn, but only if they can answer two great questions:

1. What does this part of the Bible tell me about Jesus—who He is and what He is like?
2. How does this information apply to my own life—here and now, today?

CHAPTER 2

THE GODHEAD

Have you ever wrestled with trying to understand the Trinity—the three Persons of the Godhead? How can we worship one God, when that God is three Persons? Is God a committee? No, because if God were a committee, the three members would each have their own differing ideas, opinions, and perspectives. But between the members of the Godhead, there are NO differences, except in the roles They fill in saving us from sin. They are one in heart, in mind, and in knowledge. Let us open His Word to us and learn more!

One God—but three persons?

ONE GOD:

"Hear, O Israel: The Lord our God, the Lord is one!" —Deuteronomy 6:4.

ONE LORD—ONE GOD:

"There is one body and one Spirit, just as you were called in one hope of your calling; one Lord, one faith, one baptism; one God and Father of all, who is above all, and through all, and in you all." —Ephesians 4:4–6.

THREE PERSONS: FATHER, SON, AND HOLY SPIRIT:

"Go therefore and make disciples of all the nations, baptizing them in the name of the Father and of the Son and of the Holy Spirit." —Matthew 28:19.

"The grace of the Lord Jesus Christ, and the love of God, and the communion of the Holy Spirit be with you all." —2 Corinthians 13:14.

"To the … elect according to the foreknowledge of God the Father, in sanctification of the Spirit, for obedience and sprinkling of the blood of Jesus Christ." —1 Peter 1:1, 2.

What can we know of God the Father?

HIS CHARACTER, HIS ESSENCE, IS LOVE:

"He who does not love does not know God, for God is love." —1 John 4:8.

"And the Lord passed before him and proclaimed, 'The Lord, the Lord God, merciful and gracious, longsuffering, and abounding in goodness and truth, keeping mercy for thousands, forgiving iniquity and transgression and sin.'" —Exodus 34:6, 7.

HIS LOVE GIVES—AND SAVES:

"For God so loved the world that He gave His only begotten Son, that whoever believes in Him should not perish but have everlasting life." —John 3:16.

JESUS REVEALED THE FATHER:

"He who has seen Me has seen the Father." —John 14:9.

What can we know of God the Son?

JESUS—THE WORD AND CREATOR—IS GOD:

"In the beginning was the Word, and the Word was with God, and the Word was God. He was in the beginning with God. All things were made through Him, and without Him nothing was made that was made." — John 1:1–3.

"He is the image of the invisible God, the firstborn over all creation. For by Him all things were created that are in heaven and that are on earth." —Colossians 1:15, 16.

JESUS THE WORD CAME TO LIVE AMONG US ON EARTH:

"And the Word became flesh and dwelt among us, and we beheld His glory, the glory as of the only begotten of the Father, full of grace and truth." —John 1:14.

JESUS SAID HE IS ONE WITH THE FATHER:

"I and My Father are one." —John 10:30.

IN HIS GREAT PRAYER, JESUS DESCRIBED HIS UNITY WITH THE FATHER:

"As You sent Me into the world, I also have sent them into the world. And for their sakes I sanctify Myself, that they also may be sanctified by the truth. I do not pray for these alone, but also for those who will believe in Me through their word; that they all may be one, as You, Father, are in Me, and I in You; that they also may be one in Us, that the world may believe that You sent Me. And the glory which You gave Me I have given them, that they may be one just as We are one: I in them, and You in Me; that they may be made perfect in one, and that the world may know that You have sent Me, and have loved them as You have loved Me. Father, I desire that they also

How Do You View God the Father?

Many of us see God the Father through the lens of our experience with our own earthly father. If the father figure of our childhood and youth was loving and fair and cared for us, it's easier for us to see our heavenly Father in much the same way.

But perhaps your father was abusive and unfair—or perhaps distant or even absent, physically or emotionally. So for you, maybe it's hard to see God the Father as being very much different.

Add to that the fact that Satan the great enemy of God is committed to making God look harsh, judgmental, vindictive, and even violent. Even God's own people often see God this way.

But what the devil says God is like should not be of most importance to any of us. Neither should what religions say He is like. What's of most importance is this:

WHAT DO ***YOU*** THINK GOD IS LIKE?

It's the purpose of this book to share the truth about God—to do as Jesus did when He was here: reveal the truth about the Father's unconditional, constant, forgiving, strong yet gentle love for you. Let the Bible show you who He is!

A Question

How would you feel if you knew with absolute certainty that you ***never*** need to fear God?

whom You gave Me may be with Me where I am, that they may behold My glory which You have given Me; for You loved Me before the foundation of the world. O righteous Father! The world has not known You, but I have known You; and these have known that You sent Me. And I have declared to them Your name, and will declare it, that the love with which You loved Me may be in them, and I in them." —John 17:18–26.

Jesus the Son—and You

The Bible has just shared with us that Jesus is one with the Father. Jesus was the Creator. He is God's Word, speaking to us constantly. He came to live with us, becoming a human being as we are. He spent His time here revealing the Father's character of love to us. And finally, He demonstrated just how much He loved us by giving His life to save us from the penalty of our sins.

Jesus was resurrected and returned to heaven. He lives! And He wants now more than anything to build a personal relationship with us.

With you!

Do you have time, or make time, to get better acquainted with the One who thinks of you 24/7/365? Do you know HOW to get to know Him?

By talking to Him.

And by listening to Him.

We each can talk with Jesus any time in our busy days, by praying. He eagerly listens and answers.

And He shares His truth and love with us in the pages of His Word—the Bible.

What can we know of God the Spirit?

JESUS PROMISED THE SPIRIT TO TAKE HIS PLACE ON EARTH:

"And I will pray the Father, and He will give you another Helper, that He may abide with you forever—the Spirit of truth, whom the world cannot receive, because it neither sees Him nor knows Him; but you know Him, for He dwells with you and will be in you. I will not leave you orphans; I will come to you." —John 14:16–18.

JUST AS JESUS REVEALS THE FATHER, THE SPIRIT REVEALS JESUS:

"But when the Helper comes, whom I shall send to you from the Father, the Spirit of truth who proceeds from the Father, He will testify of Me." —John 15:26.

THE SPIRIT CONVICTS OF SIN:

"Nevertheless I tell you the truth. It is to your advantage that I go away; for if I do not go away, the Helper will not come to you; but if I depart, I will send Him to you. And when He has come, He will convict the world of sin, and of righteousness, and of judgment." —John 16:7, 8.

THE SPIRIT REVEALS TRUTH TO US:

"However, when He, the Spirit of truth, has come, He will guide you into all truth; for He will not speak on His own authority, but whatever He hears He will speak; and He will tell you things to come." —John 16:13.

Can We Also Know the Holy Spirit?

The Holy Spirit may not seem as well-known to us as God the Father or Jesus the Son. But He is the same as the Father and Son in His love for us and in His desire to help us escape sin and spend eternity in heaven.

When Jesus left this earth, He gave us the gift of the Holy Spirit. And while Jesus lived WITH us, the Spirit was given to live IN us! Imagine—God Himself, living in us during our busy days. God—living in us despite our sinfulness and weakness.

The Spirit brings God's power to convict us of sin, to bring us to repentance, to break the hold of sin over us, and to help us live the life of Jesus so long as we invite the Spirit to live in us.

That power of the Spirit is unlimited. What seems impossible to us is completely possible when the Spirit is in our lives.

Another wonderful thing the Spirit can do for us is "translate" or "interpret" our prayers. We sometimes feel so deeply we can't find words to pray eloquent prayers. But the Spirit reads our hearts and presents our real desires to God the Father and God the Son in ways we never could.

Jesus came to reveal the Father. The Holy Spirit has come to reveal Jesus. What a joy it is to invite the Spirit to live in us at the start of each new day, then enjoy His revelation of Jesus to us and His power to break the power of sin in our lives.

Someday, in a world restored to its original perfection, we can be with the Godhead in person. But because of the Spirit's presence, we really don't have to wait!

CHAPTER 3

HOW Evil BEGAN

Imagine—if possible—a place utterly unlike our world. A place where absolutely no evil, no sin, no selfishness exists. A place with no pain, no tears, no death. A place instead of joy and peace and perfect health. Has such a place ever really existed? God's Word, the Bible, says yes! That place was called heaven. And for ages and ages, its inhabitants—the Godhead and the angels—delighted in heaven's perfection. Until a day of tragedy beyond all words, when sin arose in the heart of heaven's highest angel.

With whom did sin originate?

"You were the anointed cherub who covers; I established you; you were on the holy mountain of God; you walked back and forth in the midst of fiery stones. You were perfect in your ways from the day you were created, till iniquity was found in you.

"By the abundance of your trading, you became filled with violence within, and you sinned; therefore I cast you as a profane thing out of the mountain of God; and I destroyed you, O covering cherub, from the midst of the fiery stones. Your heart was lifted up because of your beauty; you corrupted your wisdom for the sake of your splendor; I cast you to the ground, I laid you before kings, that they might gaze at you.

"You defiled your sanctuaries by the multitude of your iniquities, by the iniquity of your trading; therefore I brought fire from your midst; it devoured you, and I turned you to ashes upon the earth in the sight of all who saw you." —Ezekiel 28:14–18.

"He who sins is of the devil, for the devil has sinned from the beginning." —1 John 3:8.

"You are of your father the devil, and the desires of your father you want to do. He was a murderer from the beginning, and does not stand in the truth, because there is no truth in him. When he speaks a lie, he speaks from his own resources, for he is a liar and the father of it." —John 8:44.

What one word gave rise to sin?

A WORD OF A SINGLE LETTER:

"How you are fallen from heaven, O Lucifer, son of the morning! How you are cut down to the ground, you who weakened the nations! For you have said in your heart: 'I will ascend into heaven, I will exalt my throne above the stars of God; I will also sit on the mount of the congregation on the farthest sides of the north; I will ascend above the heights of the clouds, I will be like the Most High.' " —Isaiah 14:12–14.

"I" Trouble

The verse from Isaiah above says that sin began when Lucifer began to center his life and his thoughts—not on God—but on himself.

I will ascend… *I* will exalt… *I* will also sit…

I will ascend…*I* will be like the Most High.

Yes—"I" trouble. Pride. Self-exaltation. A desire to brush God aside and be his own god.

And once Lucifer, who became Satan the dragon, was cast out of heaven, he brought the deadly virus of selfishness to earth, where he infected the perfect human beings God had created.

Ever since, we have been born with that same selfishness and pride.

It is the source of all pain, all wars, all tears, all misery, all death. It is deadly. This earth, for now, is a demonstration to the universe of what sin does.

But Satan's end is coming. And with him, the end of sin and selfishness, forever.

What was Christ's exact opposite spirit?

CHRIST, "who, being in the form of God, did not consider it robbery to be equal with God, but made Himself of no reputation, taking the form of a bondservant, and coming in the likeness of men. And being found in appearance as a man, He humbled Himself and became obedient to the point of death, even the death of the cross." —Philippians 2:6–8.

What a Contrast!

In sharp contrast with Satan's desire to lift himself higher and higher, the verse above says that the Spirit of Christ in saving us was to lower Himself down far enough to reach us.

- Down—making Himself of no reputation.
- Down—Taking the form of a servant.
- Down—Coming in the likeness of men.
- Down—He humbled Himself.
- Down—He became obedient, even to death on the cross.

In our world, it's accepted that people will do whatever it takes to get to the top, even if it means stepping over others on the way. But that's not the humble spirit of Jesus.

When the Spirit takes control of our lives, we'll want not the highest place—to be first and be noticed—but to take the place of a servant. And that spirit can be ours just by inviting the Spirit in.

Where did Lucifer's rebellion lead?

"And war broke out in heaven: Michael and his angels fought with the dragon; and the dragon and his angels fought, but they did not prevail, nor was a place found for them in heaven any longer. So the great dragon was cast out, that serpent of old, called the Devil and Satan, who deceives the whole world; he was cast to the earth, and his angels were cast out with him." —Revelation 12:7–9.

AND THE BIBLE SAYS OF THE DRAGON (SATAN):

"His tail drew a third of the stars of heaven and threw them to the earth." —Revelation 12:4.

CHAPTER 4

CREATION AND THE FALL OF MAN

Imagine a time when not a single man or woman existed—a time when even earth itself did not yet exist. Then, through the limitless creative power of His words alone, God spoke the world into existence. Then, in a single week of creation, He called forth light and seas and animals and plants, and then He crowned His creation by bringing to life the first man and woman. All was perfect. But tragically, a time came when the first human beings listened to the lies of God's sworn enemy and chose their own way rather than God's.

How did our world come to be?

THROUGH THE LIMITLESS POWER OF GOD:

"In the beginning God created the heavens and the earth." —Genesis 1:1.

BY HIS WORD ALONE: "By the word of the Lord the heavens were made, and all the host of them by the breath of His mouth. … For He spoke, and it was done; He commanded, and it stood fast." —Psalm 33:6, 9.

"By faith we understand that the worlds were framed by the word of God, so that the things which are seen were not made of things which are visible." —Hebrews 11:3.

What did God create on each day of Creation Week?

Day One: *Light*

"Then God said, 'Let there be light'; and there was light. And God saw the light, that it was good; and God divided the light from the darkness. God called the light Day, and the darkness He called Night. So the evening and the morning were the first day." —Genesis 1:3–5.

Day Two: *The Firmament, or Sky*

"Then God said, 'Let there be a firmament in the midst of the waters, and let it divide the waters from the waters.' Thus God made the firmament, and divided the waters which were under the firmament from the waters which were above the firmament; and it was so. And God called the firmament Heaven. So the evening and the morning were the second day." —Genesis 1:6–8.

Day Three: ***Lands, Seas, Plants***

"Then God said, 'Let the waters under the heavens be gathered together into one place, and let the dry land appear'; and it was so. And God called the dry land Earth, and the gathering together of the waters He called Seas. And God saw that it was good.

"Then God said, 'Let the earth bring forth grass, the herb that yields seed, and the fruit tree that yields fruit according to its kind, whose seed is in itself, on the earth'; and it was so. And the earth brought forth grass, the herb that yields seed according to its kind, and the tree that yields fruit, whose seed is in itself according to its kind. And God saw that it was good." So the evening and the morning were the third day." —Genesis 1:9–13.

Day Four: ***Sun and Moon; Stars Also***

"Then God said, 'Let there be lights in the firmament of the heavens to divide the day from the night; and let them be for signs and seasons, and for days and years; and let them be for lights in the firmament of the heavens to give light on the earth; and it was so. Then God made two great lights: the greater light to rule the day, and the lesser light to rule the night. He made the stars also. God set them in the firmament of the heavens to give light on the earth, and to rule over the day and over the night, and to divide the light from the darkness. And God saw that it was good. So the evening and the morning were the fourth day.' " —Genesis 1:14–19.

Day Five: ***Sea Life and Birds***

"Then God said, 'Let the waters abound with an abundance of living creatures, and let birds fly above the earth across the face of the firmament of the heavens.' So God created great sea creatures and every living thing that moves, with which the waters abounded, according to their kind, and every winged bird according to its kind. And God saw that it was good. And God blessed them, saying, 'Be fruitful and multiply, and fill the waters in the seas, and let birds multiply on the earth.' So the evening and the morning were the fifth day." —Genesis 1:20–23.

Day Six: ***Animals, Insects, Man***

"Then God said, 'Let the earth bring forth the living creature according to its kind: cattle and creeping thing and beast of the earth, each according to its kind'; and it was so. And God made the beast of the earth according to its kind, cattle according to its kind, and everything that creeps on the earth according to its kind. And God saw that it was good.

"Then God said, 'Let Us make man in Our image, according to Our likeness; let them have dominion over the fish of the sea, over the birds of the air, and over the cattle, over all the earth and over every creeping thing that creeps on the earth.' So God created man in His own image; in the image of God He created him; male and female He created them. Then God blessed them, and God said to them, 'Be fruitful and multiply; fill the earth and subdue it; have dominion over the fish of the sea, over the birds of the air, and over every living thing that moves on the earth.' " —Genesis 1:24–28.

Day Seven: ***The Seventh Day Sabbath of Rest***

"Thus the heavens and the earth, and all the host of them, were finished. And on the seventh day God ended His work which He had done, and He rested on the seventh day from all His work which He had done. Then God blessed the seventh day and sanctified it, because in it He rested from all His work which God had created and made." —Genesis 2:1–3.

What happened to the perfect world God created?

Sadly, tragically, the perfect earth God created was soon plunged into the horror that follows infection with the deadly virus of sin—of selfishness.

In Chapter 3 of this book, we learned how the perfection of heaven itself was shattered when sin—self-centeredness—arose in the heart of Lucifer, heaven's highest angel.

This led to war in heaven, resulting in the ejection of Lucifer and one-third of heaven's angels who followed him. Lucifer, now called Satan, was cast out and set up his headquarters on the newly created

Earth. He was determined to win the perfect man and woman—Adam and Eve—to his selfish principle in defiance of God's principle of love.

Alas, Genesis 3 tells the horrific story of his success at winning over human beings in his alliance against God. Read here that sorrowful story: "Now the serpent was more cunning than any beast of the field which the Lord God had made. And he said to the woman, 'Has God indeed said, "You shall not eat of every tree of the garden"?'

"And the woman said to the serpent, 'We may eat the fruit of the trees of the garden; but of the fruit of the tree which is in the midst of the garden, God has said, "You shall not eat it, nor shall you touch it, lest you die."'

"Then the serpent said to the woman, 'You will not surely die. For God knows that in the day you eat of it your eyes will be opened, and you will be like God, knowing good and evil.'

"So when the woman saw that the tree was good for food, that it was pleasant to the eyes, and a tree desirable to make one wise, she took of its fruit and ate. She also gave to her husband with her, and he ate. Then the eyes of both of them were opened, and they knew that they were naked; and they sewed fig leaves together and made themselves coverings.

"And they heard the sound of the Lord God walking in the garden in the cool of the day, and Adam and his wife hid themselves from the presence of the Lord God among the trees of the garden.

"Then the Lord God called to Adam and said to him, 'Where are you?'

"So he said, 'I heard Your voice in the garden, and I was afraid because I was naked; and I hid myself.'

"And He said, 'Who told you that you were naked? Have you eaten from the tree of which I commanded you that you should not eat?'

"Then the man said, 'The woman whom You gave to be with me, she gave me of the tree, and I ate.'

"And the Lord God said to the woman, 'What is this you have done?'

"The woman said, 'The serpent deceived me, and I ate.'

"So the Lord God said to the serpent: 'Because you have done this, you are cursed more than all cattle, and more than every beast of the field; on your belly you shall go, and you shall eat dust all the days of your life. And I will put enmity between you and the woman, and between your seed and her Seed; He shall bruise your head, and you shall bruise His heel.'

"To the woman He said: 'I will greatly multiply your sorrow and your conception; in pain you shall bring forth children; your desire shall be for your husband, and he shall rule over you.'

"Then to Adam He said, 'Because you have heeded the voice of your wife, and have eaten from the tree of which I commanded you, saying, "You shall not eat of it": Cursed is the ground for your sake; in toil you shall eat of it all the days of your life. Both thorns and thistles it shall bring forth for you, and you shall eat the herb of the field. In the sweat of your face you shall eat bread till you return to the ground, for out of it you were taken; for dust you are, and to dust you shall return.'

"And Adam called his wife's name Eve, because she was the mother of all living. Also for Adam and his wife the Lord God made tunics of skin, and clothed them.

"Then the Lord God said, 'Behold, the man has become like one of Us, to know good and evil. And now, lest he put out his hand and take also of the tree of life, and eat, and live forever'—therefore the Lord God sent him out of the garden of Eden to till the ground from which he was taken. So He drove out the man; and He placed cherubim at the east of the garden of Eden, and a flaming sword which turned every way, to guard the way to the tree of life." —Genesis 3:1–24.

Two Lessons We Can Learn from the Fall

No. 1: Blaming

When God asked Adam what had happened after he sinned, he blamed Eve, his wife.

When God asked Eve what had happened, she blamed the serpent—which ultimately was putting the blame on God.

Part of how sin works is to deflect blame from oneself to others. Notice how many people caught in a crime plead "not guilty." Notice how many small children blame a brother or sister for something they themselves have done.

If you ever find yourself blaming someone else for what you have done, that's evidence of sin in your life.

No 2: Fear

"Where are you, Adam?" God asked.

"I ran away and hid," he replied, "because I was afraid."

Adam—afraid of God? Before sinning, he had never feared God. Just as the Bible says that perfect love casts out fear, so too does fear cast out love. They are like oil and water—they don't mix.

If you ever find yourself afraid of God—afraid that He is like an angry judge out to catch you in your sins and punish you for them, that's fear talking. The only way to change that view of God is to expose yourself more and more to His love.

God's love WILL cast out your fear. You will come to see that He is on your side—that He is *for* you, not *against* you!

Personal Thought Questions to Consider

God could have prevented sin from ever happening, simply by not giving His created beings the gift of free will—of freedom to choose. He could have programmed both angels and human beings so they could only choose His way.

The advantage would be that sin could never have arisen. But the enormous disadvantage would be that God's created beings would have obeyed and worshiped Him, not from love, but because they had no choice in the matter.

In your opinion, was the risk of free will worth it?

☐ Yes
☐ No

Why?______________________________

"If you eat of this fruit," the devil said, "your eyes will be opened to understand great things." His implication was that God was holding out on Adam and Eve—not sharing certain kinds of elevated spiritual knowledge.

Can you see that Satan still uses that argument today? Do you think it's possible that this is the attraction of such belief systems as:

- The New Age (including "The Secret")
- Scientology
- Mormonism
- Christian Science
- Freemasonry
- Emerging Church/Spiritual Formation
- Spiritualism
- Eastern Religions

Write a few of your thoughts concerning the above:______________________________

____

____

____

CHAPTER 5

THE PLAN OF SALVATION

For this and the following two chapters, we are going to look at three priceless gifts God gave us from Eden. Even though His perfect creation was marred when Adam and Eve fell into sin, His love continued to surround those He had created.

Once we sinned, we were truly doomed. That would have been the end of us but for the love of God, which already had in reserve a plan to save us from sin's consequence of death. Let us now consider this first gift of Eden together.

Where did sin leave us?

IN ADAM, WE ALL SINNED:

"Therefore, just as through one man sin entered the world, and death through sin, and thus death spread to all men, because all sinned." —Romans 5:12.

"For all have sinned and fall short of the glory of God." —Romans 3:23.

"For the wages of sin is death, but the gift of God is eternal life in Christ Jesus our Lord." —Romans 6:23.

How does God plan to save us?

God's Plan has two parts—His part and our part. We need to clearly understand the difference.

OUR SALVATION: *GOD'S PART*

ONE OF THE BIBLE'S MOST-LOVED VERSES: "For God so loved the world that He gave His only begotten Son, that whoever believes in Him should not perish but have everlasting life." —John 3:16.

"But God demonstrates His own love toward us, in that while we were still sinners, Christ died for us." — Romans 5:8.

"For as in Adam all die, even so in Christ all shall be made alive." —1 Corinthians 15:22.

"For by grace you have been saved through faith, and that not of yourselves; it is the gift of God, not of works, lest anyone should boast." —Ephesians 2:8, 9.

Have You?

Have you accepted the sacrifice of Jesus on the cross for you as your only hope of salvation?

If not, why delay? Why not now?

"Today, if you will hear His voice, do not harden your hearts."—Hebrews 3:15.

OUR SALVATION: ***OUR PART***

"But as many as received Him, to them He gave the right to become children of God, to those who believe in His name." —John 1:12.

"Behold, I stand at the door and knock. If anyone hears My voice and opens the door, I will come in to him and dine with him, and he with Me." —Revelation 3:20.

"And this is the testimony: that God has given us eternal life, and this life is in His Son. He who has the Son has life; he who does not have the Son of God does not have life. These things I have written to you who believe in the name of the Son of God, that you may know that you have eternal life, and that you may continue to believe in the name of the Son of God." — 1 John 5:11–13.

Confusing God's part and our part in salvation

From the very beginning, Satan has done his best to confuse men and women concerning the difference between what God does to save us— and what we do.

At the cross Jesus finished the work of our salvation on our behalf.

- We cannot add to it.
- We cannot earn it.
- We cannot deserve it.
- We can contribute nothing to it by our good works or good behavior.

Our salvation is all of Christ—and as the verses from Ephesians in the opposite column make plain, our salvation is a gift, pure and simple. No one "earns" a gift. No one "pays" for a gift. All we can do is accept that gift in gratitude.

We are saved when we trust that Christ's perfect life and His death as our Substitute is sufficient for us.

- Trusting is our part.
- Accepting is our part.
- Being sure of our salvation is our part.

But, so many ask, does trusting in God's finished work of saving us release us from living Christ-like lives and obeying Him?

Not at all. Because when we accept Jesus as our Saviour, we also accept Him as our Lord—to live His life in and through us. Note this:

"I have been crucified with Christ; it is no longer I who live, but Christ lives in me; and the life which I now live in the flesh I live by faith in the Son of God, who loved me and gave Himself for me." —Galatians 2:20.

I can't save myself. And I can't live as I should. But Jesus can do both! This is why the gospel of salvation is called Good News!

CHAPTER 6

ENTERING INTO GOD'S REST

The second of the three great gifts God gave us from Eden is the seventh-day Sabbath. And what a gift it is! Not only does it provide a weekly rest from our physical labors—our jobs, vocations, and clocking in and out each day, but it has an even greater significance.

For the Sabbath is not just a chance to rest from our daily labor; it is also a symbol of the rest that is ours from the labor of trying to be good enough to save. We can rest in His finished work, because Jesus has done the work of saving us, we can rest in His finished work.

Which day is God's Sabbath?

THE LORD HAS A DAY:

"I was in the Spirit on the Lord's Day, and I heard behind me a loud voice, as of a trumpet." —Revelation 1:10.

HIS DAY IS THE SABBATH:

"Therefore the Son of Man is also Lord of the Sabbath." —Mark 2:28.

THE SEVENTH DAY IS THE SABBATH:

"But the seventh day is the Sabbath of the Lord your God." —Exodus 20:10.

THE SEVENTH-DAY SABBATH WAS CREATED ON THE SEVENTH DAY OF CREATION WEEK:

"Then God blessed the seventh day and sanctified it, because in it He rested from all His work which God had created and made." —Genesis 2:3.

What is the Sabbath Commandment?

THE FOURTH OF GOD'S TEN COMMANDMENTS:

"Remember the Sabbath day, to keep it holy. Six days you shall labor and do all your work, but the seventh day is the Sabbath of the Lord your God. In it you shall do no work: you, nor your son, nor your daughter, nor your male servant, nor your female servant, nor your cattle, nor your stranger who is within your gates. For in six days the Lord made the heavens and the earth, the sea, and all that is in them, and rested the seventh day. Therefore the Lord blessed the Sabbath day and hallowed it." —Exodus 20:8–11.

What is the significance of the Sabbath?

A SIGN OF RESTING FROM OUR OWN WORKS:

"For He has spoken in a certain place of the seventh day in this way: 'And God rested on the seventh day from all His works.' ... There remains therefore a rest for the people of God. For he who has entered His rest has himself also ceased from his works as God did from His. Let us therefore be diligent to enter that rest." —Hebrews 4:4, 9–11.

A SIGN OF SANCTIFICATION:

"Speak also to the children of Israel, saying: 'Surely My Sabbaths you shall keep, for it is a sign between Me and you throughout your generations, that you may know that I am the Lord who sanctifies you.'" —Exodus 31:13.

"Moreover I also gave them My Sabbaths, to be a sign between them and Me, that they might know that I am the Lord who sanctifies them. ... Hallow My Sabbaths, and they will be a sign between Me and you, that you may know that I am the Lord your God." —Ezekiel 20:12, 20.

What the Sabbath Celebrates

In the verses above, the Bible shows us that the Sabbath celebrates three things:

1. It is a weekly reminder of God's creation, as noted in the fourth commandment.
2. It is a reminder too that we can rest from our own works to be saved, since Jesus has already accomplished that for us at the cross.
3. It is a reminder that Jesus also sanctifies us—that is, He lives in us through His Holy Spirit and makes us like Himself.

What is the history of Sabbathkeeping?

ISRAEL KEPT THE SABBATH BEFORE THE LAW WAS GIVEN AT SINAI:

"And so it was, on the sixth day, that they gathered twice as much bread, two omers for each one. And all the rulers of the congregation came and told Moses. Then he said to them, 'This is what the Lord has said: "Tomorrow is a Sabbath rest, a holy Sabbath to the Lord. Bake what you will bake today, and boil what you will boil; and lay up for yourselves all that remains, to be kept until morning."'" —Exodus 16:22, 23.

JESUS KEPT THE SABBATH:

"So He came to Nazareth, where He had been brought up. And as His custom was, He went into the synagogue on the Sabbath day, and stood up to read." —Luke 4:16.

PAUL KEPT THE SABBATH:

"And he reasoned in the synagogue every Sabbath, and persuaded both Jews and Greeks." —Acts 18:4.

THE SABBATH WILL BE KEPT IN THE NEW EARTH:

"'And it shall come to pass that from one New Moon to another, and from one Sabbath to another, all flesh shall come to worship before Me,' says the Lord." —Isaiah 66:23.

How shall we keep the Sabbath?

"If you turn away your foot from the Sabbath, from doing your pleasure on My holy day, and call the Sabbath a delight, the holy day of the Lord honorable, and shall honor Him, not doing your own ways, nor finding your own pleasure, nor speaking your own words, then you shall delight yourself in the Lord; and I will cause you to ride on the high hills of the earth, and feed you with the heritage of Jacob your father. The mouth of the Lord has spoken." —Isaiah 58:13, 14.

"And He said to them, 'The Sabbath was made for man, and not man for the Sabbath.' "—Mark 2:27.

"It is lawful to do good on the Sabbath." —Matthew 12:12.

"And behold, there was a certain man before Him who had dropsy. And Jesus, answering, spoke to the lawyers and Pharisees, saying, 'Is it lawful to heal on the Sabbath?' … And He took him and healed him, and let him go. Then He answered them, saying, 'Which of you, having a donkey or an ox that has fallen into a pit, will not immediately pull him out on the Sabbath day?' "—Luke 14:2–5.

When shall we observe the Sabbath?

FRIDAY IS THE "PREPARATION DAY" BEFORE THE SABBATH:

"Therefore, because it was the Preparation Day, that the bodies should not remain on the cross on the Sabbath (for that Sabbath was a high day), the Jews asked Pilate that their legs might be broken, and that they might be taken away." —John 19:31.

SABBATH TO BE CELEBRATED FROM EVENING TO EVENING:

"It shall be to you a sabbath of solemn rest, and you shall afflict your souls; on the ninth day of the month at evening, from evening to evening, you shall celebrate your sabbath." —Leviticus 23:32.

"EVENING" IS WHEN THE SUN SETS:

"At evening, when the sun had set, they brought to Him all who were sick and those who were demon-possessed." —Mark 1:32.

"Happy Sabbath!"

Many Sabbathkeepers enjoy greeting one another with these words on the Sabbath day, or as it approaches.

Likewise, many Jewish Sabbathkeepers greet one another with "Shabbat Shalom" ("Sabbath of Peace").

Seventh-day Adventist Sabbathkeepers typically welcome the Sabbath on Friday evening at sunset, then attend Sabbath services on Saturday morning (Sabbath School—a time for group study of the Bible—and the worship hour).

As the Bible says, "Not forsaking the assembling of ourselves together, as is the manner of some; but exhorting one another, and so much the more as you see the Day approaching." —Hebrews 10:25.

CHAPTER 7

Marriage, Family, and the Home

We now arrive at the third of God's great gifts from Eden: Marriage, the Family, and the Home. As God created it, marriage was to be a priceless blessing to human beings—and from those marriages, children would be added to form the intimacy and love of a peaceful home.

Once sin invaded our earth, marriage and the family came under Satan's aggressive, focused attacks. As we discover God's plan for marriage and families, we can even today enjoy much of the heaven it was designed to bring us.

When did marriage begin?

"And the Lord God said, 'It is not good that man should be alone; I will make him a helper comparable to him.' Out of the ground the Lord God formed every beast of the field and every bird of the air, and brought them to Adam to see what he would call them. And whatever Adam called each living creature, that was its name. So Adam gave names to all cattle, to the birds of the air, and to every beast of the field. But for Adam there was not found a helper comparable to him. And the Lord God caused a deep sleep to fall on Adam, and he slept; and He took one of his ribs, and closed up the flesh in its place. Then the rib which the Lord God had taken from man He made into a woman, and He brought her to the man. And Adam said: 'This is now bone of my bones and flesh of my flesh; she shall be called Woman, because she was taken out of Man.' Therefore a man shall leave his father and mother and be joined to his wife, and they shall become one flesh. And they were both naked, the man and his wife, and were not ashamed." —Genesis 2:18–25.

Did Jesus celebrate marriage when He was here on Earth?

"On the third day there was a wedding in Cana of Galilee, and the mother of Jesus was there. Now both Jesus and His disciples were invited to the wedding. And when they ran out of wine, the mother of Jesus said to Him, 'They have no wine.' Jesus said to her, 'Woman, what does your concern have to do with Me? My hour has not yet come.' His mother said to the servants, 'Whatever He says to you, do it.'

"Now there were set there six waterpots of stone, according to the manner of purification of the Jews, containing twenty or thirty gallons apiece. Jesus said to them, 'Fill the waterpots with water.' And they filled them up to the brim. And He said to them, 'Draw some out now, and take it to the master of the feast.' And they took it. When the master of the feast had tasted the water that was made wine, and did not know where it came from (but the servants who had drawn the water knew), the master of the feast called the bridegroom. And he said to him, 'Every man at the beginning sets out the good wine, and when the guests have well drunk, then the inferior. You have kept the good wine until now!' This beginning of signs Jesus did in Cana of Galilee, and manifested His glory; and His disciples believed in Him."—John 2:1–11.

Marriage as Jesus Created It

The creator intended that this magnificent gift from Eden should be an enormous blessing to the men and women He created.

As He created it, marriage was to be a union of one man and one woman. In recent years, however, society has increasingly accepted the idea of marriage between members of the same sex.

In view of what the Bible says, how do you feel about this? ______________________________

____

____

____

What does the Bible say about how to have a happy marriage?

HOW WIVES ARE TO RELATE TO THEIR HUSBANDS:

"Wives, submit to your own husbands, as to the Lord. For the husband is head of the wife, as also Christ is head of the church; and He is the Savior of the body. Therefore, just as the church is subject to Christ, so let the wives be to their own husbands in everything." —Ephesians 5:22–24.

HOW HUSBANDS ARE TO RELATE TO THEIR WIVES:

"Husbands, love your wives, just as Christ also loved the church and gave Himself for her, that He might sanctify and cleanse her with the washing of water by the word, that He might present her to Himself a glorious church, not having spot or wrinkle or any such thing, but that she should be holy and without blemish. So husbands ought to love their own wives as their own bodies; he who loves his wife loves himself. For no one ever hated his own flesh, but nourishes and cherishes it, just as the Lord does the church. For we are members of His body, of His flesh and of His bones." —Ephesians 5:25–30.

COUPLES SHOULD LEAVE THEIR PARENTS AND BECOME ONE FLESH TOGETHER:

"For this reason a man shall leave his father and mother and be joined to his wife, and the two shall become one flesh." —Ephesians 5:31.

COUPLES SHOULD DEMONSTRATE MUTUAL LOVE AND RESPECT:

"Nevertheless let each one of you in particular so love his own wife as himself, and let the wife see that she respects her husband." —Ephesians 5:33.

BELIEVERS SHOULD MARRY BELIEVERS:

"Do not be unequally yoked together with unbelievers. For what fellowship has righteousness with lawlessness? And what communion has light with darkness?" —2 Corinthians 6:14.

What did Jesus teach about divorce?

RECONCILIATION, NOT DIVORCE, IS GOD'S WILL:

"Now to the married I command, yet not I but the Lord: A wife is not to depart from her husband. But even if she does depart, let her remain unmarried or be reconciled to her husband. And a husband is not to divorce his wife." —1 Corinthians 7:10, 11.

JESUS TEACHES ABOUT DIVORCE:

"Furthermore it has been said, 'Whoever divorces his wife, let him give her a certificate of divorce.' But I say to you that whoever divorces his wife for any reason except sexual immorality causes her to commit adultery; and whoever marries a woman who is divorced commits adultery." —Matthew 5:31, 32.

JESUS AGAIN TEACHES ABOUT DIVORCE:

"The Pharisees also came to Him, testing Him, and saying to Him, 'Is it lawful for a man to divorce his wife for just any reason?' And He answered and said to them, 'Have you not read that He who made them at the beginning "made them male and female," and said, "For this reason a man shall leave his father and mother and be joined to his wife, and the two shall become one flesh"? So then, they are no longer two but one flesh. Therefore what God has joined together, let not man separate.' They said to Him, 'Why then did Moses command to give a certificate of divorce, and to put her away?' He said to them, 'Moses, because of the hardness of your hearts, permitted you to divorce your wives, but from the beginning it was not so. And I say to you, whoever divorces his wife, except for sexual immorality, and marries another, commits adultery; and whoever marries her who is divorced commits adultery.'" —Matthew 19:3–9.

MARRIAGE IN HEAVEN?

In one of their many efforts to "trap" Jesus, the religious leaders (Pharisees) came to Him one day and presented the hypothetical scenario of a woman who had been married multiple times, surviving each of her several husbands.

"So whose wife will she be in the resurrection?" they asked.

"Jesus answered and said to them, 'You are mistaken, not knowing the Scriptures nor the power of God. For in the resurrection they neither marry nor are given in marriage, but are like angels of God in heaven.'"—Matthew 22:29, 30.

This thought is troubling to many who have been married more than once. But consider this: If everything in eternity will be better than what we have on earth, can't we trust God to have something far BETTER than marriage waiting for us?

What does the Bible have to say about children and child-rearing?

CHILDREN ARE TO OBEY AND HONOR THEIR PARENTS:

"Children, obey your parents in the Lord, for this is right. 'Honor your father and mother,' which is the first commandment with promise: 'that it may be well with you and you may live long on the earth.'" —Ephesians 6:1–3.

FATHERS TO TRAIN THEIR CHILDREN AS GUIDED BY THE LORD:

"And you, fathers, do not provoke your children to wrath, but bring them up in the training and admonition of the Lord."—Ephesians 6:4.

PARENTS TO TEACH CHILDREN GOD'S LAW AND WILL:

"And these words which I command you today shall be in your heart. You shall teach them diligently to your children, and shall talk of them when you sit in your house, when you walk by the way, when you lie down, and when you rise up. You shall bind them as a sign on your hand, and they shall be as frontlets between your eyes. You shall write them on the doorposts of your house and on your gates."—Deuteronomy 6:6–9.

GOD'S PROMISE TO PARENTS:

"Train up a child in the way he should go, and when he is old he will not depart from it." —Proverbs 22:6.

CHAPTER 8

GOD'S LAW—AND HIS GRACE

Some look at God's law and see it as a list of rules—rules that not only limit personal freedom but are virtually impossible to keep. As some have pointed out, God's law is simply the written expression of His character of love. How, then, could it possibly be against us?

Sin, the Bible says, is breaking the law. We are all sinners. The good news is that God's grace—His love—provides both the antidote for sin and the empowerment needed to obey His law.

Did God's Law exist before Sinai?

GOD'S LAW IS ETERNAL:

"All His precepts [commandments] are sure. They stand fast forever and ever." —Psalm 111:7, 8.

PAUL SHOWS THAT THE LAW EXISTED FROM EDEN:

"Therefore, just as through one man sin entered the world, and death through sin, and thus death spread to all men, because all sinned—(For until the law sin was in the world, but sin is not imputed when there is no law. Nevertheless death reigned from Adam to Moses, even over those who had not sinned according to the likeness of the transgression of Adam, who is a type of Him who was to come.)" —Romans 5:12–14.

ABRAHAM KEPT GOD'S LAW BEFORE SINAI:

"Because Abraham obeyed My voice and kept My charge, My commandments, My statutes, and My laws." —Genesis 26:5.

THE SABBATH COMMANDMENT EXISTED BEFORE GIVEN AT SINAI:

"So they laid it [manna] up till morning, as Moses commanded; and it did not stink, nor were there any worms in it. Then Moses said, 'Eat that today, for today is a Sabbath to the Lord; today you will not find it in the field. Six days you shall gather it, but on the seventh day, the Sabbath, there will be none.'

"Now it happened that some of the people went out on the seventh day to gather, but they found none. And the Lord said to Moses, 'How long do you refuse to keep My commandments and My laws? See! For the Lord has given you the Sabbath; therefore He gives you on the sixth day bread for two days. Let every man remain in his place; let no man go out of his place on the seventh day.' So the people rested on the seventh day." —Exodus 16:24–30.

What does God's Ten-Commandment Law include?

THE TEN COMMANDMENTS THAT GOD GAVE TO MOSES AT SINAI:

"You shall have no other gods before Me.

"You shall not make for yourself a carved image—any likeness of anything that is in heaven above, or that is in the earth beneath, or that is in the water under the earth; you shall not bow down to them nor serve them. For I, the Lord your God, am a jealous God, visiting the iniquity of the fathers upon the children to the third and fourth generations of those who hate Me, but showing mercy to thousands, to those who love Me and keep My commandments.

"You shall not take the name of the Lord your God in vain, for the Lord will not hold him guiltless who takes His name in vain.

"Remember the Sabbath day, to keep it holy. Six days you shall labor and do all your work, but the seventh day is the Sabbath of the Lord your God. In it you shall do no work: you, nor your son, nor your daughter, nor your male servant, nor your female servant, nor your cattle, nor your stranger who is within your gates. For in six days the Lord made the

heavens and the earth, the sea, and all that is in them, and rested the seventh day. Therefore the Lord blessed the Sabbath day and hallowed it.

"Honor your father and your mother, that your days may be long upon the land which the Lord your God is giving you.

"You shall not murder.

"You shall not commit adultery.

"You shall not steal.

"You shall not bear false witness against your neighbor.

"You shall not covet your neighbor's house; you shall not covet your neighbor's wife, nor his male servant, nor his female servant, nor his ox, nor his donkey, nor anything that is your neighbor's." — Exodus 20:3–17.

What else does the Bible have to say about God's law?

GOD'S LAW IS PERFECT:

"The law of the Lord is perfect, converting the soul; the testimony of the Lord is sure, making wise the simple." —Psalm 19:7.

OBEYING THE LAW DOES NOT JUSTIFY US; BUT IT DOES POINT OUT SIN:

"Therefore by the deeds of the law no flesh will be justified in His sight, for by the law is the knowledge of sin." —Romans 3:20.

SIN IS BREAKING THE LAW:

"Whoever commits sin also commits lawlessness, and sin is lawlessness." —1 John 3:4.

KNOWING TO DO RIGHT BUT NOT DOING IT IS SIN:

"Therefore, to him who knows to do good and does not do it, to him it is sin." —James 4:17.

How does God's law show itself in our daily living?

JESUS SUMMARIZED THE TEN COMMANDMENTS DOWN TO JUST TWO—LOVE FOR GOD AND LOVE FOR MAN:

" 'Teacher, which is the great commandment in the law?'

"Jesus said to him, 'You shall love the Lord your God with all your heart, with all your soul, and with all your mind.' This is the first and great commandment. And the second is like it: 'You shall love your neighbor as yourself.' On these two commandments hang all the Law and the Prophets." —Matthew 22:36–40.

BLESSINGS OF OBEYING GOD'S LAW:

"Now it shall come to pass, if you diligently obey the voice of the Lord your God, to observe carefully all His commandments which I command you today, that the Lord your God will set you high above all nations of the earth. And all these blessings shall come upon you and overtake you, because you obey the voice of the Lord your God." —Deuteronomy 28:1, 2.

GOD'S NEW COVENANT: HIS LAW INSIDE US—IN OUR MINDS AND HEARTS:

"Behold, the days are coming, says the Lord, when I will make a new covenant with the house of Israel and with the house of Judah—not according to the covenant that I made with their fathers in the day that I took them by the hand to lead them out of the land of Egypt, My covenant which they broke, though I was a husband to them, says the Lord. But this is the covenant that I will make with the house of Israel after those days, says the Lord: I will put My law in their minds, and write it on their hearts; and I will be their God, and they shall be My people." —Jeremiah 31:31–33.

GOD'S LAW IS NOT A BURDEN:

"For this is the love of God, that we keep His commandments. And His commandments are not burdensome." —1 John 5:3.

How did Jesus relate to the Law while here?

JESUS KEPT HIS FATHER'S COMMANDMENTS:

"If you keep My commandments, you will abide in My love, just as I have kept My Father's commandments and abide in His love." —John 15:10.

JESUS URGES HIS FOLLOWERS TO KEEP THEM TOO:

"If you love Me, keep My commandments." —John 14:15.

JESUS CAME TO FULFILL HIS LAW, NOT TO DESTROY IT:

"Do not think that I came to destroy the Law or the Prophets. I did not come to destroy but to fulfill. For assuredly, I say to you, till heaven and earth pass away, one jot or one tittle will by no means pass from the law till all is fulfilled." —Matthew 5:17, 18.

SOMETHING WAS NAILED TO THE CROSS:

"And you, being dead in your trespasses and the uncircumcision of your flesh, He has made alive together with Him, having forgiven you all trespasses, having wiped out the handwriting of requirements that was against us, which was contrary to us. And He has taken it out of the way, having nailed it to the cross." —Colossians 2:13, 14.

IT WAS THE CEREMONIAL LAW—NOT THE TEN-COMMANDMENT LAW—THAT WAS NAILED TO THE CROSS:

"Having abolished in His flesh the enmity, that is, the law of commandments contained in ordinances, so as to create in Himself one new man from the two, thus making peace." —Ephesians 2:15.

Did the Law continue after Jesus returned to heaven?

PAUL SAID IT WAS STILL IN EFFECT:

"Therefore the law is holy, and the commandment holy and just and good." —Romans 7:12.

SO DID JOHN:

"He who says, 'I know Him,' and does not keep His commandments, is a liar, and the truth is not in him." —1 John 2:4.

Two Ways to Keep God's Law

After God gave His people the Ten Commandment law, they confidently replied, "All the words which the Lord has said we will do. —Exodus 24:3.

They failed miserably. They broke their agreement, or covenant, with God. As the Bible says in the text above from Jeremiah, God made a new covenant with them.

The difference?

Under the old covenant, God's people tried to keep His law as a set of external rules—as a duty, an obligation, a burden.

Under the new covenant, God placed His law in their very heart of hearts, so that now they wanted to keep His law—they found its requirements a joy instead of a burden.

The old covenant was rules only. The new covenant was the joyful heart response of people in love with God.

How does law relate to grace?

WE ARE UNDER GRACE, BUT THAT IS NOT A LICENSE TO SIN:

"For sin shall not have dominion over you, for you are not under law but under grace. What then? Shall we sin because we are not under law but under grace? Certainly not!" —Romans 6:14, 15.

FUNCTION OF THE LAW TO REVEAL SIN CONTINUES AFTER THE CROSS:

"But be doers of the word, and not hearers only, deceiving yourselves. For if anyone is a hearer of the word and not a doer, he is like a man observing his natural face in a mirror; for he observes himself, goes away, and immediately forgets what kind of man he was. But he who looks into the perfect law of liberty and continues in it, and is not a forgetful hearer but a doer of the work, this one will be blessed in what he does." —James 1:22–25.

DUTY TO KEEP THE LAW CONTINUES AFTER THE CROSS:

"Now by this we know that we know Him, if we keep His commandments." —1 John 2:3.

FAITH IN GOD'S GRACE DOES NOT RELEASE US FROM KEEPING THE LAW:

"Do we then make void the law through faith? Certainly not! On the contrary, we establish the law." —Romans 3:31.

PAUL DELIGHTED TO KEEP THE LAW:

"For I delight in the law of God according to the inward man." —Romans 7:22.

NEW-COVENANT LAW-KEEPING—THE OBEDIENCE OF GRACE:

"For this is the covenant that I will make with the house of Israel after those days, says the Lord: I will put My laws in their mind and write them on their hearts; and I will be their God, and they shall be My people." —Hebrews 8:10.

CHAPTER 9

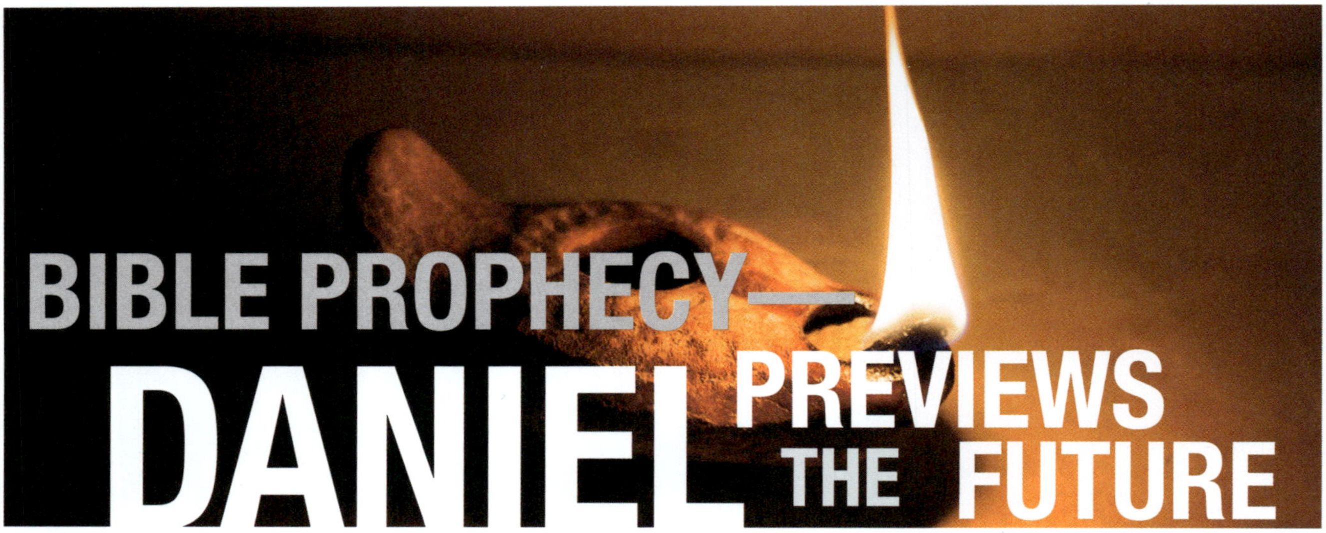

BIBLE PROPHECY—DANIEL PREVIEWS THE FUTURE

Image by www.istockphoto.com.

God tells us in His Word that He does nothing of great historical significance without sharing His plans in advance through His prophets. Using amazing images and symbols, the Old Testament book of Daniel (and its companion prophetic Bible book of Revelation), details world events from the time of the prophet Daniel until the Second Coming of Jesus. These captivating prophecies give sincere Bible students inside information on God's plans for His people and for our world.

Does God reveal the future to us?

"Surely the Lord God does nothing, unless He reveals His secret to His servants the prophets." —Amos 3:7.

"Behold, the former things have come to pass, and new things I declare; before they spring forth I tell you of them." —Isaiah 42:9.

"Remember the former things of old, for I am God, and there is no other; I am God, and there is none like Me, declaring the end from the beginning, and from ancient times things that are not yet done." —Isaiah 46:9, 10.

"For prophecy never came by the will of man, but holy men of God spoke as they were moved by the Holy Spirit." —2 Peter 1:21.

Some Key Bible Prophecies

Found in the Old Testament book of Daniel and the New Testament book of Revelation are many prophecies revealing future events. In this chapter, we will briefly look at two of those:

- Daniel 2
- Daniel 7

Then, in the next chapter, we will focus on the Bible's longest time prophecy found in Daniel 8.

What does God reveal in Daniel 2?

FOUR GREAT KINGDOMS

From the time of Babylon's King Nebuchadnezzar in 603 B.C. to the Second Coming of Jesus—yet future—God showed through His prophet Daniel that four great kingdoms would reign on earth, followed by a splintering of the final kingdom into ten parts.

After his dream, what did King Nebuchanezzar say to his wise men?

"And the king said to them, 'I have had a dream, and my spirit is anxious to know the dream.'" —Daniel 2:3.

And the conversation that followed?

"Then the Chaldeans spoke to the king in Aramaic, 'O king, live forever! Tell your servants the dream, and we will give the interpretation.'

"The king answered and said to the Chaldeans, 'My decision is firm: if you do not make known the dream to me, and its interpretation, you shall be cut in pieces, and your houses shall be made an ash heap. However, if you tell the dream and its interpretation, you shall receive from me gifts, rewards, and great honor. Therefore tell me the dream and its interpretation.'

"They answered again and said, 'Let the king tell his servants the dream, and we will give its interpretation.'" —Daniel 2:4–7.

Were the Wise Men Able to Satisfy the King?

"The king answered and said, 'I know for certain that you would gain time, because you see that my decision is firm: if you do not make known the dream to me, there is only one decree for you! For you have agreed to speak lying and corrupt words before me till the time has changed. Therefore tell me the dream, and I shall know that you can give me its interpretation.'

"The Chaldeans answered the king, and said, 'There is not a man on earth who can tell the king's matter; therefore no king, lord, or ruler has ever asked such things of any magician, astrologer, or Chaldean. It is a difficult thing that the king requests, and there is no other who can tell it to the king except the gods, whose dwelling is not with flesh.'

"For this reason the king was angry and very furious, and gave the command to destroy all the wise men of Babylon. So the decree went out, and they began killing the wise men; and they sought Daniel and his companions, to kill them." —Daniel 2:8–13.

What happened when Daniel learned of the king's request?

"Then with counsel and wisdom Daniel answered Arioch, the captain of the king's guard, who had gone out to kill the wise men of Babylon; he answered and said to Arioch the king's captain, 'Why is the decree from the king so urgent?' Then Arioch made the decision known to Daniel.

"So Daniel went in and asked the king to give him time, that he might tell the king the interpretation. Then Daniel went to his house, and made the decision known to Hananiah, Mishael, and Azariah, his companions, that they might seek mercies from the God of heaven concerning this secret, so that Daniel and his companions might not perish with the rest of the wise men of Babylon. Then the secret was revealed to Daniel in a night vision. So Daniel blessed the God of heaven." —Daniel 2:14–19.

What promise did Daniel take to the king?

"Therefore Daniel went to Arioch, whom the king had appointed to destroy the wise men of Babylon. He went and said thus to him: 'Do not destroy the wise men of Babylon; take me before the king, and I will tell the king the interpretation.'

"Then Arioch quickly brought Daniel before the king, and said thus to him, 'I have found a man of the captives of Judah, who will make known to the king the interpretation.'

"The king answered and said to Daniel, whose name was Belteshazzar, 'Are you able to make known to me the dream which I have seen, and its interpretation?'

“Daniel answered in the presence of the king, and said, ‘The secret which the king has demanded, the wise men, the astrologers, the magicians, and the soothsayers cannot declare to the king. But there is a God in heaven who reveals secrets, and He has made known to King Nebuchadnezzar what will be in the latter days. Your dream, and the visions of your head upon your bed, were these: As for you, O king, thoughts came to your mind while on your bed, about what would come to pass after this; and He who reveals secrets has made known to you what will be. But as for me, this secret has not been revealed to me because I have more wisdom than anyone living, but for our sakes who make known the interpretation to the king, and that you may know the thoughts of your heart.’ ”—Daniel 2:24–30.

What dream did Daniel reveal to the king?

"You, O king, were watching; and behold, a great image! This great image, whose splendor was excellent, stood before you; and its form was awesome. This image's head was of fine gold, its chest and arms of silver, its belly and thighs of bronze, its legs of iron, its feet partly of iron and partly of clay. You watched while a stone was cut out without hands, which struck the image on its feet of iron and clay, and broke them in pieces. Then the iron, the clay, the bronze, the silver, and the gold were crushed together, and became like chaff from the summer threshing floors; the wind carried them away so that no trace of them was found. And the stone that struck the image became a great mountain and filled the whole earth."—Daniel 2:31–35.

Image by Remnant Publications.

What Interpretation did Daniel share next?

"This is the dream. Now we will tell the interpretation of it before the king. You, O king, are a king of kings. For the God of heaven has given you a kingdom, power, strength, and glory; and wherever the children of men dwell, or the beasts of the field and the birds of the heaven, He has given them into your hand, and has made you ruler over them all—you are this head of gold. But after you shall arise another kingdom inferior to yours; then another, a third kingdom of bronze, which shall rule over all the earth. And the fourth kingdom shall be as strong as iron, inasmuch as iron breaks in pieces and shatters everything; and like iron that crushes, that kingdom will break in pieces and crush all the others. Whereas you saw the feet and toes, partly of potter's clay and partly of iron, the kingdom shall be divided; yet the strength of the iron shall be in it, just as you saw the iron mixed with ceramic clay. And as the toes of the feet were partly of iron and partly of clay, so the kingdom shall be partly strong and partly fragile. As you saw iron mixed with ceramic clay, they will mingle with the seed of men; but they will not adhere to one another, just as iron does not mix with clay. And in the days of these kings the God of heaven will set up a kingdom which shall never be destroyed; and the kingdom shall not be left to other people; it shall break in pieces and consume all these kingdoms, and it shall stand forever. Inasmuch as you saw that the stone was cut out of the mountain without hands, and that it broke in pieces the iron, the bronze, the clay, the silver, and the gold—the great God has made known to the king what will come to pass after this. The dream is certain, and its interpretation is sure."—Daniel 2:36–45.

Did the King's Dream Come to Pass?

Yes—in every detail. See Nebuchadnezzar's great image on the facing page—along with the historical dates of each kingdom.

What does God reveal in Daniel 7?

Again: Four Great Kingdoms

Whereas in Daniel 2, the world's present and future great kingdoms were represented by parts of the image Nebuchadnezzar dreamed about, in Daniel 7 those kingdoms were shown to Daniel as four great beasts. The two prophecies are best studied together to note the parallels.

What was Daniel's chapter 7 vision?

"In the first year of Belshazzar king of Babylon, Daniel had a dream and visions of his head while on his bed. Then he wrote down the dream, telling the main facts.

"Daniel spoke, saying, 'I saw in my vision by night, and behold, the four winds of heaven were stirring up the Great Sea. And four great beasts came up from the sea, each different from the other. The first was like a lion, and had eagle's wings. I watched till its wings were plucked off; and it was lifted up from the earth and made to stand on two feet like a man, and a man's heart was given to it.

" 'And suddenly another beast, a second, like a bear. It was raised up on one side, and had three ribs in its mouth between its teeth. And they said thus to it: "Arise, devour much flesh!"

" 'After this I looked, and there was another, like a leopard, which had on its back four wings of a bird. The beast also had four heads, and dominion was given to it.

" 'After this I saw in the night visions, and behold, a fourth beast, dreadful and terrible, exceedingly strong. It had huge iron teeth; it was devouring, breaking in pieces, and trampling the residue with its feet. It was different from all the beasts that were before it, and it had ten horns. I was considering the horns, and there was another horn, a little one, coming up among them, before whom three of the first horns were plucked out by the roots. And there, in this horn, were eyes like the eyes of a man, and a mouth speaking pompous words.'

" 'I watched till thrones were put in place, and the Ancient of Days was seated; His garment was white as snow, and the hair of His head was like pure wool. His throne was a fiery flame, its wheels a burning fire; a fiery stream issued and came forth from before Him. A thousand thousands ministered to Him; ten thousand times ten thousand stood before Him. The court was seated, and the books were opened.

" 'I watched then because of the sound of the pompous words which the horn was speaking; I watched till the beast was slain, and its body destroyed and given to the burning flame. As for the rest of the beasts, they had their dominion taken away, yet their lives were prolonged for a season and a time.

" 'I was watching in the night visions, and behold, One like the Son of Man, coming with the clouds of heaven! He came to the Ancient of Days, and they brought Him near before Him. Then to Him was given dominion and glory and a kingdom, that all peoples, nations, and languages should serve Him.

" 'His dominion is an everlasting dominion, which shall not pass away, and His kingdom the one which shall not be destroyed.' " —Daniel 7:1–14.

And what was the interpretation?

"I, Daniel, was grieved in my spirit within my body, and the visions of my head troubled me. I came near to one of those who stood by, and asked him the truth of all this. So he told me and made known to me the interpretation of these things: 'Those great beasts, which are four, are four kings which arise out of the earth. But the saints of the Most High shall receive the kingdom, and possess the kingdom forever, even forever and ever.'

"Then I wished to know the truth about the fourth beast, which was different from all the others, exceedingly dreadful, with its teeth of iron and its nails of bronze, which devoured, broke in pieces, and trampled the residue with its feet; and the ten horns that were on its head, and the other horn which came up, before which three fell, namely, that horn which had eyes and a mouth which spoke pompous words, whose appearance was greater than his fellows.

"I was watching; and the same horn was making war against the saints, and prevailing against them, until the Ancient of Days came, and a judgment was made in favor of the saints of the Most High, and the time came for the saints to possess the kingdom.

"Thus he said: 'The fourth beast shall be a fourth kingdom on earth, which shall be different from all other kingdoms, and shall devour the whole earth, trample it and break it in pieces. The ten horns are ten kings who shall arise from this kingdom. And another shall rise after them; he shall be different from the first ones, and shall subdue three kings. He shall speak pompous words against the Most High, shall persecute the saints of the Most High, and shall intend to change times and law. Then the saints shall be given into his hand for a time and times and half a time. But the court shall be seated, and they shall take away his dominion, to consume and destroy it forever. Then the kingdom and dominion, and the greatness of the kingdoms under the whole heaven, shall be given to the people, the saints of the Most High. His kingdom is an everlasting kingdom, and all dominions shall serve and obey Him.

"This is the end of the account. As for me, Daniel, my thoughts greatly troubled me, and my countenance changed; but I kept the matter in my heart."
—Daniel 7:15–28.

Image by Present Solutions. Used with permission.

Image by Present Solutions. Used with permission.

Image by Present Solutions. Used with permission.

Image by Present Solutions. Used with permission.

CHAPTER 10

THE BIBLE'S LONGEST TIME PROPHECY

After the amazing vision of the Four Beasts in Daniel 7, the prophet records in Daniel 8 and 9 yet another striking vision he was shown.

He wrote of seeing a ram and a goat, of a "little horn," and shared a prophecy covering more time than any other in all the Bible—2,300 years!

This great vision was shown to Daniel in the year 538 B.C.—the same year in which the Kingdom of Babylon fell.

What did Daniel see as his chapter 8 vision began?

"In the third year of the reign of King Belshazzar a vision appeared to me—to me, Daniel—after the one that appeared to me the first time. I saw in the vision, and it so happened while I was looking, that I was in Shushan, the citadel, which is in the province of Elam; and I saw in the vision that I was by the River Ulai. Then I lifted my eyes and saw, and there, standing beside the river, was a ram which had two horns, and the two horns were high; but one was higher than the other, and the higher one came up last. I saw the ram pushing westward, northward, and southward, so that no animal could withstand him; nor was there any that could deliver from his hand, but he did according to his will and became great." —Daniel 8:1–4.

What did the ram represent?

DANIEL'S ANGEL GUIDE IN THE VISION TOLD HIM THE MEANING OF THE SYMBOL:

"The ram which you saw, having the two horns—they are the kings of Media and Persia." —Daniel 8:20.

What did Daniel see next?

"And as I was considering, suddenly a male goat came from the west, across the surface of the whole earth, without touching the ground; and the goat had a notable horn between his eyes. Then he came to the ram that had two horns, which I had seen standing beside the river, and ran at him with furious power." —Daniel 8:5, 6.

And what did this goat represent?

"And the male goat is the kingdom of Greece. The large horn that is between its eyes is the first king. As for the broken horn and the four that stood up in its place, four kingdoms shall arise out of that nation, but not with its power." —Daniel 8:21, 22.

What was the "large horn," and what happened when it was broken?

The Large Horn and the Four That Stood Up in Its Place

From history, it's clear that the "large horn" on the male goat represented Alexander the Great, who led the forces of Greece in defeating Medo-Persia in 331 B.C. A few years after Alexander died in 323, the kingdom was divided among his four leading generals: Cassander, Lysimachus, Ptolemy, and Seleucus.

The large horn was broken, but standing up in its (Alexander's) place were the four monarchies of the generals, each of whom assumed the title of "king."

What rose up from one of the four horns?

"And out of one of them came a little horn which grew exceedingly great toward the south, toward the east, and toward the Glorious Land. And it grew up to the host of heaven; and it cast down some of the host and some of the stars to the ground, and trampled them. He even exalted himself as high as the Prince of the host; and by him the daily sacrifices were taken away, and the place of His sanctuary was cast down. Because of transgression, an army was given over to the horn to oppose the daily sacrifices; and he cast truth down to the ground. He did all this and prospered." —Daniel 8:9–12.

How is the little horn power described?

"And in the latter time of their kingdom, when the transgressors have reached their fullness, a king shall arise, having fierce features, who understands sinister schemes. His power shall be mighty, but not by his own power; he shall destroy fearfully, and shall prosper and thrive; he shall destroy the mighty, and also the holy people.

"Through his cunning he shall cause deceit to prosper under his rule; and he shall exalt himself in his heart. He shall destroy many in their prosperity.

He shall even rise against the Prince of princes; but he shall be broken without human means.

"And the vision of the evenings and mornings which was told is true; therefore seal up the vision, for it refers to many days in the future." —Daniel 8:23–26.

Can we know the identity of the little horn power?

"The interpretation already given to this vision shows plainly that the power represented by the little horn is the successor of Medo-Persia and Grecia. In the vision of the seventh chapter of Daniel, which is closely related to this vision, the fourth beast represented the fourth kingdom, or Rome, in its entirety, special attention, however, being given to the 'little horn' phase of its history. As shown by the work attributed to it, this little horn, which arose among the ten kingdoms into which Rome was divided, was to be a religio-political power, which was to change the times and law of God, and persecute the people of God. In the vision of the eighth chapter the ecclesiastical features of this fourth world power are especially noticed and emphasized, and hence the only symbol there used to represent it is the 'little horn' which waxed 'exceeding great.'

"The religion of all the four great monarchies mentioned in these prophecies was paganism; but the paganism of ancient Babylon was reproduced in pagan Rome, and then adapted and adopted by papal Rome. The little horn of the eighth chapter represents Rome, both pagan and papal, in its ecclesiastical aspect, with its union of paganism, and later of apostate Christianity, with the secular power; with its antichristian persecutions of the saints of God; with its perversion of the priesthood of Christ and with its assertion of both temporal and spiritual power over all the world. It is evident that pagan Rome is introduced into this prophecy chiefly as a means of locating the place and work of papal Rome, and the ecclesiastical features of pagan Rome as typical of the same features accentuated in papal Rome, and that the emphasis is to be placed upon the fulfillment of the prophecy in the work of papal Rome. A careful comparison of Dan. 7:21, 25, with Dan. 8:10–12, R.V., and 2 Thess. 2:3, 4, will amply justify this conclusion." —P. V. N. Myers, *Rome, Its Rise and Fall* (Boston: Ginn and Co., 1901), 398, 399.

NOTE: Many historians agree with Myers in identifying the Little Horn Power as papal Rome as it rose to power in the context of pagan Rome.

What did Daniel hear next in the vision?

"Then I heard a holy one speaking; and another holy one said to that certain one who was speaking, 'How long will the vision be, concerning the daily sacrifices and the transgression of desolation, the giving of both the sanctuary and the host to be trampled underfoot?'

"And he said to me, 'For two thousand three hundred days; then the sanctuary shall be cleansed.' " —Daniel 8:13, 14.

Before this long prophecy could be explained, what happened to Daniel?

"And I, Daniel, fainted and was sick for days; afterward I arose and went about the king's business. I was astonished by the vision, but no one understood it." —Daniel 8:27.

Why Are Daniel's Prophecies Important to Study?

- Because God loves us enough to tell us ahead of time what is coming here on earth.
- Because we need to know enough that we will not be deceived by misinformation or caught unprepared by lack of information.
- Because we learn through fulfilled prophecy that we can trust God implicitly.

Later when Daniel felt better, who appeared to him to explain the vision?

"Now while I was speaking, praying, and confessing my sin and the sin of my people Israel, and presenting my supplication before the Lord my God for the holy mountain of my God, yes, while I was speaking in prayer, the man Gabriel, whom I had seen in the vision at the beginning, being caused to fly swiftly, reached me about the time of the evening offering. And he informed me, and talked with me, and said, 'O Daniel, I have now come forth to give you skill to understand. At the beginning of your supplications the command went out, and I have come to tell you, for you are greatly beloved; therefore consider the matter, and understand the vision."—Daniel 9:20–23.

NOTE: Comparative Bible study supports the conclusion that Gabriel was a heavenly angel. Some believe he took the place of the fallen Lucifer as heaven's chief angel.

With what time period did Gabriel begin his explanation?

"Seventy weeks are determined [in the original language of the Bible, the word determined also means "cut off"] for your people and for your holy city, to finish the transgression, to make an end of sins, to make reconciliation for iniquity, to bring in everlasting righteousness, to seal up vision and prophecy, and to anoint the Most Holy.

"Know therefore and understand, that from the going forth of the command to restore and build Jerusalem until Messiah the Prince, there shall be seven weeks and sixty-two weeks; the street shall be built again, and the wall, even in troublesome times.

"And after the sixty-two weeks Messiah shall be cut off, but not for Himself; and the people of the prince who is to come shall destroy the city and the sanctuary. The end of it shall be with a flood, and till the end of the war desolations are determined.

"Then He shall confirm a covenant with many for one week; but in the middle of the week He shall bring an end to sacrifice and offering. And on the wing of abominations shall be one who makes desolate, even until the consummation, which is determined, is poured out on the desolate." —Daniel 9:24–27.

What prophetic key helps us understand Bible-time prophecies?

A DAY IN PROPHETIC TIME EQUALS A YEAR:

"According to the number of the days in which you spied out the land, forty days, for each day you shall bear your guilt one year, namely forty years, and you shall know My rejection."—Numbers 14:34.

"And when you have completed them, lie again on your right side; then you shall bear the iniquity of the house of Judah forty days. I have laid on you a day for each year."—Ezekiel 4:6.

When did the 70-week prophecy begin?

NOTE: As already stated in Daniel 9:24, the 70 weeks were "cut off" from … what? Clearly, from an even longer time period. And the only longer period mentioned earlier was the 2,300 days of Daniel 8:14.

Daniel 9:25 says the 70 weeks began at the "going forth of the command to restore and build Jerusalem." History confirms that this command was given by Artaxerxes in 457 B.C.

Therefore, the beginning date for the 70 weeks—and thus for the 2,300 days, was 457 B.C.

What happened at the end of the 2,300-day prophecy?

"For two thousand three hundred days; then the sanctuary shall be cleansed."—Daniel 8:14, emphasis supplied.

NOTE: Students of prophecy are largely in agreement that the "sanctuary" here is the Heavenly Sanctuary, after which the Old Testament wilderness sanctuary was modeled.

Seventh-day Adventists and some other prophetic scholars believe that at the end of the 2,300 days (years) in 1844, Jesus entered the Heavenly Sanctuary to cleanse it of its record of sin—just as the Old Testament prophets performed the same work in the desert sanctuary.

See the chart of the 2,300-day prophecy below.

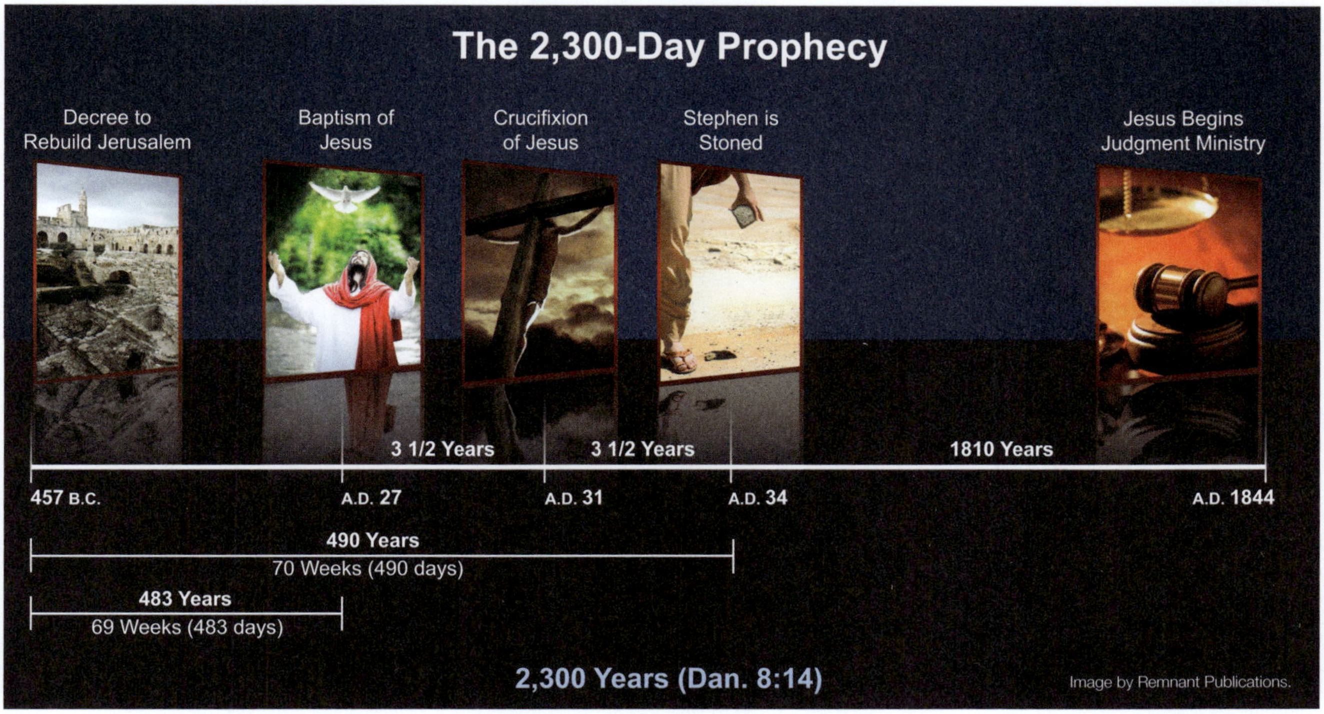

CHAPTER 11

THE BIRTH, LIFE, AND MINISTRY OF JESUS

Without Him, there would be no Bible. Without Him, there would be no Christian Church. Without Him as Creator, our world and universe would not exist. Without Him as Savior, we would all be without hope—destined for everlasting death.

But Jesus LIVES! He is both God and Man—and He came to our sin-damaged world to save us—to give us another chance at eternal life. The Bible tells the story of His birth, His life and ministry, and above all, His love.

Was the coming of Jesus to earth predicted?

WHAT GOD SAID TO SATAN IN EDEN (IN THE FORM OF A SERPENT):

"So the Lord God said to the serpent: Because you have done this, you are cursed more than all cattle, and more than every beast of the field; on your belly you shall go, and you shall eat dust all the days of your life. And I will put enmity between you and the woman [the Church], and between your seed and her Seed [Jesus Christ]; He shall bruise your head, and you shall bruise His heel." —Genesis 3:14, 15.

"But you, Bethlehem Ephrathah, though you are little among the thousands of Judah, yet out of you shall come forth to Me the One to be Ruler in Israel, whose goings forth are from of old, from everlasting." —Micah 5:2.

"Therefore the Lord Himself will give you a sign: Behold, the virgin shall conceive and bear a Son, and shall call His name Immanuel." —Isaiah 7:14.

"For unto us a Child is born, unto us a Son is given; and the government will be upon His shoulder. And His name will be called Wonderful, Counselor, Mighty God, Everlasting Father, Prince of Peace. Of the increase of His government and peace there will be no end, upon the throne of David and over His kingdom, to order it and establish it with judgment and justice from that time forward, even forever. The zeal of the Lord of hosts will perform this." —Isaiah 9:6, 7.

What does the Bible say about the birth of Jesus?

MATTHEW'S RECORD:

"Now the birth of Jesus Christ was as follows: After His mother Mary was betrothed to Joseph, before they came together, she was found with child of the Holy Spirit. Then Joseph her husband, being a just man, and not wanting to make her a public example, was minded to put her away secretly. But while he thought about these things, behold, an angel of the Lord appeared to him in a dream, saying, 'Joseph, son of David, do not be afraid to take to you Mary your wife, for that which is conceived in her is of the Holy Spirit. And she will bring forth a Son, and you shall call His name Jesus, for He will save His people from their sins.'" —Matthew 1:18–21.

LUKE'S RECORD:

"Then the angel said to them, 'Do not be afraid, for behold, I bring you good tidings of great joy which will be to all people. For there is born to you this day in the city of David a Savior, who is Christ the Lord. And this will be the sign to you: You will find a Babe wrapped in swaddling cloths, lying in a manger.'

"And suddenly there was with the angel a multitude of the heavenly host praising God and saying: 'Glory to God in the highest, and on earth peace, goodwill toward men!' So it was, when the angels had gone away from them into heaven, that the shepherds said to one another, 'Let us now go to Bethlehem and see this thing that has come to pass, which the Lord has made known to us.' And they came with haste and found Mary and Joseph, and the Babe lying in a manger." —Luke 2:10–16.

JESUS GREW PHYSICALLY AND INTELLECTUALLY:

"And the Child grew and became strong in spirit, filled with wisdom; and the grace of God was upon Him." —Luke 2:40.

AT 12 YEARS OF AGE, JESUS RECOGNIZED HIS MISSION:

"And when He was twelve years old, they went up to Jerusalem according to the custom of the feast. When they had finished the days, as they returned, the Boy Jesus lingered behind in Jerusalem. And Joseph and His mother did not know it; but supposing Him to have been in the company, they went a day's journey, and sought Him among their relatives and acquaintances. So when they did not find Him, they returned to Jerusalem, seeking Him. Now so it was that after three days they found Him in the temple, sitting in the midst of the teachers, both listening to them and asking them questions. And all who heard Him were astonished at His understanding and answers. So when they saw Him, they were amazed; and His mother said to Him, 'Son, why have You done this to us? Look, Your father and I have sought You anxiously.' And He said to them, 'Why did you seek Me? Did you not know that I must be about My Father's business?'" —Luke 2:42–49.

Why Did Jesus Come to This Earth?

The Bible provides many reasons that Jesus chose to come to this earth. Check off which of the following are most personally meaningful to you.

He came to …

- Call people to repentance
- Save us from our sins
- Live a perfect life which He offers to exchange for ours
- Show us the character of God the Father
- Prepare the way for the Holy Spirit to indwell us
- Answer Satan's many lies about God and His law
- Show that the law could be fulfilled when human beings rely on divine power
- Offer us the security of salvation by His death on the cross
- Offer us life more abundantly
- Be our Source of life, truth, and light
- Do His Father's will
- Demonstrate what real love is like

CHAPTER 12

THE DEATH AND RESURRECTION OF JESUS

It is not easy to read or imagine the story of Christ's death on the cross and His resurrection two days later. Cruelty, agony, mockery, and a pain and sorrow of soul too deep for words—Jesus endured it all. This was the greatest-ever act of love, the day that made it possible for us to escape eternal death.

That weekend ended in the resurrection—where Jesus forever broke the chains of death and gave us hope of eternal life after this one is done.

How was Christ's death predicted and described?

"Who has believed our report? And to whom has the arm of the Lord been revealed? For He shall grow up before Him as a tender plant, and as a root out of dry ground. He has no form or comeliness; and when we see Him, there is no beauty that we should desire Him. He is despised and rejected by men, a Man of sorrows and acquainted with grief. And we hid, as it were, our faces from Him; He was despised, and we did not esteem Him. Surely He has borne our griefs and carried our sorrows; yet we esteemed Him stricken, smitten by God, and afflicted. But He was wounded for our transgressions, He was bruised for our iniquities; the chastisement for our peace was upon Him, and by His stripes we are healed. All we like sheep have gone astray; we have turned, every one, to his own way; and the Lord has laid on Him the iniquity of us all.He was oppressed and He was afflicted, yet He opened not His mouth; He was led as a lamb to the slaughter, and as a sheep before its shearers is silent, so He opened not His mouth. He was taken from prison and from judgment, and who will declare His generation? For He was cut off from the land of the living; for the transgressions of My people He was stricken. And they made His grave with the wicked—but with the rich at His death, because He had done no violence, nor was any deceit in His mouth." —Isaiah 53:1–9.

What did Christ's love drive Him to do for us?

"By this we know love, because He laid down His life for us. And we also ought to lay down our lives for the brethren." —1 John 3:16.

How do the Gospels describe the death of Jesus?

JOHN DESCRIBES CHRIST'S DEATH ON THE CROSS:

"And He, bearing His cross, went out to a place called the Place of a Skull, which is called in Hebrew, Golgotha, where they crucified Him, and two others with Him, one on either side, and Jesus in the center. Now Pilate wrote a title and put it on the cross. And the writing was:

JESUS OF NAZARETH, THE KING OF THE JEWS.

"Then many of the Jews read this title, for the place where Jesus was crucified was near the city; and it was written in Hebrew, Greek, and Latin.

"Therefore the chief priests of the Jews said to Pilate, 'Do not write, "The King of the Jews," but, "He said, 'I am the King of the Jews.'"

"Pilate answered, 'What I have written, I have written.'

"Then the soldiers, when they had crucified Jesus, took His garments and made four parts, to each soldier a part, and also the tunic. Now the tunic was without seam, woven from the top in one piece. They said therefore among themselves, 'Let us not tear it, but cast lots for it, whose it shall be,' that the Scripture might be fulfilled which says: 'They divided My garments among them, and for My clothing they cast lots.'

"Therefore the soldiers did these things.

"Now there stood by the cross of Jesus His mother, and His mother's sister, Mary the wife of Clopas, and Mary Magdalene. When Jesus therefore saw His mother, and the disciple whom He loved standing by, He said to His mother, 'Woman, behold your son!' Then He said to the disciple, 'Behold your mother!' And from that hour that disciple took her to his own home.

"After this, Jesus, knowing that all things were now accomplished, that the Scripture might be fulfilled, said, I thirst!' Now a vessel full of sour wine was sitting there; and they filled a sponge with sour wine, put it on hyssop, and put it to His mouth. So when Jesus had received the sour wine, He said, 'It is finished!' And bowing His head, He gave up His spirit.

"Therefore, because it was the Preparation Day, that the bodies should not remain on the cross on the Sabbath (for that Sabbath was a high day), the Jews asked Pilate that their legs might be broken, and that they might be taken away. Then the soldiers came and broke the legs of the first and of the other who was crucified with Him. But when they came to Jesus and saw that He was already dead, they did not break His legs. But one of the soldiers pierced His side with a spear, and immediately blood and water came out. And he who has seen has testified, and his testimony is true; and he knows that he is telling the truth, so that you may believe. For these things were done that the Scripture should be fulfilled, 'Not one of His bones shall be broken.' And again another Scripture says, 'They shall look on Him whom they pierced.'" —John 19:17–37.

MATTHEW DESCRIBES THE CRUCIFIXION:

"Then the soldiers of the governor took Jesus into the Praetorium and gathered the whole garrison around Him. And they stripped Him and put a scarlet robe on Him. When they had twisted a crown of thorns, they put it on His head, and a reed in His right hand. And they bowed the knee before Him and mocked Him, saying, 'Hail, King of the Jews!' Then they spat on Him, and took the reed and struck Him on the head. And when they had mocked Him, they took the robe off Him, put His own clothes on Him, and led Him away to be crucified.

"Now as they came out, they found a man of Cyrene, Simon by name. Him they compelled to bear His cross. And when they had come to a place called Golgotha, that is to say, Place of a Skull, they gave Him sour wine mingled with gall to drink. But when He had tasted it, He would not drink.

"Then they crucified Him, and divided His garments, casting lots, that it might be fulfilled which was spoken by the prophet: 'They divided My garments among them, and for My clothing they cast lots.'

"Sitting down, they kept watch over Him there. And they put up over His head the accusation written against Him:

THIS IS JESUS THE KING OF THE JEWS.

"Then two robbers were crucified with Him, one on the right and another on the left.

"And those who passed by blasphemed Him, wagging their heads and saying, 'You who destroy the temple and build it in three days, save Yourself! If You are the Son of God, come down from the cross.'

"Likewise the chief priests also, mocking with the scribes and elders, said, 'He saved others; Himself He cannot save. If He is the King of Israel, let Him now come down from the cross, and we will believe Him. He trusted in God; let Him deliver Him now if He will have Him; for He said, 'I am the Son of God.'

"Even the robbers who were crucified with Him reviled Him with the same thing.

"Now from the sixth hour until the ninth hour there was darkness over all the land. And about the ninth hour Jesus cried out with a loud voice, saying, 'Eli, Eli, lama sabachthani?' that is, 'My God, My God, why have You forsaken Me?'

"Some of those who stood there, when they heard that, said, 'This Man is calling for Elijah!' Immediately one of them ran and took a sponge, filled it with sour wine and put it on a reed, and offered it to Him to drink.

"The rest said, 'Let Him alone; let us see if Elijah will come to save Him.'

"And Jesus cried out again with a loud voice, and yielded up His spirit." —Matthew 27:27–50.

Image by www.istockphoto.com.

What happened Sunday morning after Christ's death on the cross?

"Now after the Sabbath, as the first day of the week began to dawn, Mary Magdalene and the other Mary came to see the tomb. And behold, there was a great earthquake; for an angel of the Lord descended from heaven, and came and rolled back the stone from the door, and sat on it. His countenance was like lightning, and his clothing as white as snow. And the guards shook for fear of him, and became like dead men.

"But the angel answered and said to the women, 'Do not be afraid, for I know that you seek Jesus who was crucified. He is not here; for He is risen, as He said. Come, see the place where the Lord lay. And go quickly and tell His disciples that He is risen from the dead, and indeed He is going before you into Galilee; there you will see Him. Behold, I have told you.'

"So they went out quickly from the tomb with fear and great joy, and ran to bring His disciples word.

"And as they went to tell His disciples, behold, Jesus met them, saying, 'Rejoice!' So they came and held Him by the feet and worshiped Him. Then Jesus said to them, 'Do not be afraid. Go and tell My brethren to go to Galilee, and there they will see Me.' "
—Matthew 28:1–10.

What does the resurrection mean to you and me?

"Now if Christ is preached that He has been raised from the dead, how do some among you say that there is no resurrection of the dead? But if there is no resurrection of the dead, then Christ is not risen. And if Christ is not risen, then our preaching is empty and your faith is also empty. Yes, and we are found false witnesses of God, because we have testified of God that He raised up Christ, whom He did not raise up—if in fact the dead do not rise. For if the dead do not rise, then Christ is not risen. And if Christ is not risen, your faith is futile; you are still in your sins! Then also those who have fallen asleep in Christ have perished. If in this life only we have hope in Christ, we are of all men the most pitiable.

"But now Christ is risen from the dead, and has become the firstfruits of those who have fallen asleep. For since by man came death, by Man also came the resurrection of the dead. For as in Adam all die, even so in Christ all shall be made alive. But each one in his own order: Christ the firstfruits, afterward those who are Christ's at His coming. Then comes the end, when He delivers the kingdom to God the Father, when He puts an end to all rule and all authority and power. For He must reign till He has put all enemies under His feet. The last enemy that will be destroyed is death. For 'He has put all things under His feet.' But when He says 'all things are put under Him,' it is evident that He who put all things under Him is excepted. Now when all things are made subject to Him, then the Son Himself will also be subject to Him who put all things under Him, that God may be all in all.

"Otherwise, what will they do who are baptized for the dead, if the dead do not rise at all? Why then are they baptized for the dead? And why do we stand in jeopardy every hour? I affirm, by the boasting in you which I have in Christ Jesus our Lord, I die daily. If, in the manner of men, I have fought with beasts at Ephesus, what advantage is it to me? If the dead do not rise, 'Let us eat and drink, for tomorrow we die!'

"Do not be deceived: 'Evil company corrupts good habits.' Awake to righteousness, and do not sin; for some do not have the knowledge of God. I speak this to your shame.

"But someone will say, 'How are the dead raised up? And with what body do they come?' Foolish one, what you sow is not made alive unless it dies. And what you sow, you do not sow that body that shall be, but mere grain—perhaps wheat or some other grain. But God gives it a body as He pleases, and to each seed its own body.

"All flesh is not the same flesh, but there is one kind of flesh, of men, another flesh of animals, another of fish, and another of birds.

"There are also celestial bodies and terrestrial bodies; but the glory of the celestial is one, and the glory of the terrestrial is another. There is one glory of the sun, another glory of the moon, and another glory of the stars; for one star differs from another star in glory.

"So also is the resurrection of the dead. The body is sown in corruption, it is raised in incorruption. It is sown in dishonor, it is raised in glory. It is sown in weakness, it is raised in power. It is sown a natural body, it is raised a spiritual body. There is a natural body, and there is a spiritual body. And so it is written, 'The first man Adam became a living being.' The last Adam became a life-giving spirit.

"However, the spiritual is not first, but the natural, and afterward the spiritual. The first man was of the earth, made of dust; the second Man is the Lord from heaven. As was the man of dust, so also are those who are made of dust; and as is the heavenly Man, so also are those who are heavenly. And as we have borne the image of the man of dust, we shall also bear the image of the heavenly Man.

"Now this I say, brethren, that flesh and blood cannot inherit the kingdom of God; nor does corruption inherit incorruption. Behold, I tell you a mystery: We shall not all sleep, but we shall all be changed—in a moment, in the twinkling of an eye, at the last trumpet. For the trumpet will sound, and the dead will be raised incorruptible, and we shall be changed. For this corruptible must put on incorruption, and this mortal must put on immortality. So when this corruptible has put on incorruption, and this mortal has put on immortality, then shall be brought to pass the saying that is written: 'Death is swallowed up in victory.'

"O Death, where is your sting?

O Hades, where is your victory?'

"The sting of death is sin, and the strength of sin is the law. But thanks be to God, who gives us the victory through our Lord Jesus Christ."
—1 Corinthians 15:12–57.

CHAPTER 13

CHRIST'S CHURCH AND ITS FINAL REMNANT

While here on earth, Jesus founded His Church—a band of followers, small at first but soon growing explosively—that would carry on His mission following His resurrection and ascension back to heaven. Christianity would survive and grow through the centuries, sometimes popular but sometimes persecuted.

In His Word, God predicted that soon before the return of Jesus at His Second Coming, a faithful remnant of His church would rise up with a special final message to share with the entire world.

How does the Bible say we can identify God's remnant church?

NOTE TWO IDENTIFYING MARKS:

"And the dragon [a Bible name for Satan] was enraged with the woman [God's Church], and he went to make war with the rest of her offspring [the remnant (KJV)], who keep the commandments of God and have the testimony of Jesus Christ." —Revelation 12:17.

TWO MARKS:

1) The Remnant Church "keep the commandments of God," and they

2) "Have the testimony of Jesus Christ."

And what is this "testimony of Jesus"?

"And I fell at his feet to worship him. But he said to me, "See that you do not do that! I am your fellow servant, and of your brethren who have the testimony of Jesus. Worship God! For the testimony of Jesus is the spirit of prophecy." —Revelation 19:10.

The Testimony of Jesus = The Spirit of Prophecy

Does any church today possess both marks of the remnant church?

1. KEEPING THE COMMANDMENTS OF GOD

Most churches keep at least some of God's Ten-Commandment law. A few keep nearly all of them. But even fewer keep the fourth commandment — the Sabbath as God's memorial of creation, rest, and sanctification.

And of those that keep this fourth commandment, setting apart the seventh-day Sabbath (Saturday) according to the commandment, only one keeps all the other nine, as well as possessing the second mark of God's remnant: the testimony of Jesus.

2. HAVING THE TESTIMONY OF JESUS

The Bible is its own interpreter, and in the same book of Revelation, it defines the "testimony of Jesus" as "the spirit of prophecy."

So God's remnant church will be identified both by its seventh-day Sabbathkeeping but also by its possessing of the spirit of prophecy.

This prophetic gift, Seventh-day Adventists have no doubt, was seen in the life and writings and ministry of one of its founders—Ellen G. White.

One of the most prolific authors of all time, Ellen (known by her fellow Adventists as "Sister White") wrote out her visions and messages from the Spirit to guide the young church—and her ministry continues today, even though she lived between 1827 and 1915.

Her many books still speak and guide and inspire, and, during her life she led out in establishing educational, publishing, and medical institutions that would be a marvel to the world.

Why did God need to choose and create a "remnant" of His Church? To them, He entrusted urgent messages to share with the world just prior to His Second Coming to earth.

What messages has God given to His remnant church to share?

THREE ANGELS' MESSAGES

THE FIRST ANGEL'S MESSAGE: "Then I saw another angel flying in the midst of heaven, having the everlasting gospel to preach to those who dwell on the earth—to every nation, tribe, tongue, and people—saying with a loud voice, 'Fear God and give glory to Him, for the hour of His judgment has come; and worship Him who made heaven and earth, the sea and springs of water.' " —Revelation 14:6, 7.

The First Angel's Message

SUMMARY: A call to worship God and glorify Him, "for the hour of HIS judgment has come."

Adventist prophetic scholars believe this hour arrived in 1844, at the end of the Bible's longest time prophecy: the 2,300 days.

THE SECOND ANGEL'S MESSAGE: "And another angel followed, saying, 'Babylon is fallen, is fallen, that great city, because she has made all nations drink of the wine of the wrath of her fornication.' " —Revelation 14:8.

The Second Angel's Message

SUMMARY: Using the real pagan city of Babylon (a name meaning "confusion") as a symbol of fallen religion—of apostate, error-filled, rebellious religion—the prophet says part of the threefold message of the remnant church to the world is to expose this counterfeit system of religious confusion, to help people avoid being deceived by its subtle opposition to God's truth.

THE THIRD ANGEL'S MESSAGE: "Then a third angel followed them, saying with a loud voice, 'If anyone worships the beast and his image, and receives his mark on his forehead or on his hand, he himself shall also drink of the wine of the wrath of God, which is poured out full strength into the cup of His indignation. He shall be tormented with fire and brimstone in the presence of the holy angels and in the presence of the Lamb. And the smoke of

their torment ascends forever and ever; and they have no rest day or night, who worship the beast and his image, and whoever receives the mark of his name.' "—Revelation 14:9–11.

The Third Angel's Message

SUMMARY: A direct warning against following the Beast or his image, or accepting his mark. To set forth the identity of …

- The Beast
- The Image of the Beast
- Or the Mark of the Beast

… would take many pages. Seventh-day Adventist scholars, joined by those of many other faiths, identify the Beast as the institution of the Roman papacy. The Image is formed when the United States, in the near future, links up with and gives political power to the Beast. The Mark of the Beast will be demonstrated in the papal enforcement of Sunday as the weekly rest day, in place of the Bible Sabbath.

Angels by Joe Maniscalco.

CHAPTER 14

SACRED CEREMONIES: BAPTISM AND COMMUNION

As Jesus formed His infant church—His first band of followers—He gave them two important ceremonies to remind them of His saving work FOR them—as well as IN them. He told them that He was leaving these deeply meaningful observances as examples for all His followers to continue until He returned to this earth again at His Second Coming. Those who do follow His example find that these observances keep their spiritual connection with Jesus alive during His absence.

How important is baptism to the Christian?

"And He said to them, 'Go into all the world and preach the gospel to every creature. He who believes and is baptized will be saved; but he who does not believe will be condemned.'" —Mark 16:15, 16.

"Then Jesus came from Galilee to John at the Jordan to be baptized by him. And John tried to prevent Him, saying, 'I need to be baptized by You, and are You coming to me?'

"But Jesus answered and said to him, 'Permit it to be so now, for thus it is fitting for us to fulfill all righteousness.' Then he allowed Him." —Matthew 3:13–15.

What is the spiritual symbolism of baptism?

DEATH, BURIAL, AND RESURRECTION:

"Or do you not know that as many of us as were baptized into Christ Jesus were baptized into His death? Therefore we were buried with Him through baptism into death, that just as Christ was raised from the dead by the glory of the Father, even so we also should walk in newness of life." —Romans 6:3, 4.

BURIED AND RESURRECTED:

"Buried with Him in baptism, in which you also were raised with Him through faith in the working of God, who raised Him from the dead." —Colossians 2:12.

A SYMBOL OF A NEW RELATIONSHIP WITH CHRIST:

"For as many of you as were baptized into Christ have put on Christ." —Galatians 3:27.

WE RECEIVE THE HOLY SPIRIT AT BAPTISM:

"Then Peter said to them, 'Repent, and let every one of you be baptized in the name of Jesus Christ for the remission of sins; and you shall receive the gift of the Holy Spirit.'" —Acts 2:38.

WE BECOME PART OF CHRIST'S BODY (HIS CHURCH) AT BAPTISM:

"For as the body is one and has many members,

but all the members of that one body, being many, are one body, so also is Christ. For by one Spirit we were all baptized into one body—whether Jews or Greeks, whether slaves or free—and have all been made to drink into one Spirit." —1 Corinthians 12:12, 13.

ON BEING BAPTIZED AGAIN AFTER RECEIVING NEW TRUTH:

"And it happened, while Apollos was at Corinth, that Paul, having passed through the upper regions, came to Ephesus. And finding some disciples he said to them, 'Did you receive the Holy Spirit when you believed?'

"So they said to him, 'We have not so much as heard whether there is a Holy Spirit.'

"And he said to them, 'Into what then were you baptized?'

"So they said, 'Into John's baptism.'

"Then Paul said, 'John indeed baptized with a baptism of repentance, saying to the people that they should believe on Him who would come after him, that is, on Christ Jesus.'

"When they heard this, they were baptized in the name of the Lord Jesus. And when Paul had laid hands on them, the Holy Spirit came upon them, and they spoke with tongues and prophesied. Now the men were about twelve in all." —Acts 19:1–7.

What is the correct way to be baptized?

THE EXAMPLE OF JESUS WAS TO BE IMMERSED UNDER THE WATER:

"When He had been baptized, Jesus came up immediately from the water; and behold, the heavens were opened to Him, and He saw the Spirit of God descending like a dove and alighting upon Him." —Matthew 3:16.

WHEN PHILIP BAPTIZED THE EUNUCH, THEY BOTH WENT DOWN INTO THE WATER:

"Now as they went down the road, they came to some water. And the eunuch said, 'See, here is water. What hinders me from being baptized?'

"Then Philip said, 'If you believe with all your heart, you may.'

"And he answered and said, 'I believe that Jesus Christ is the Son of God.'

"So he commanded the chariot to stand still. And both Philip and the eunuch went down into the water, and he baptized him. Now when they came up out of the water, the Spirit of the Lord caught Philip away, so that the eunuch saw him no more; and he went on his way rejoicing." —Acts 8:36–39.

Why Baptism Is So Important

- It symbolizes our death to our old life of sin and selfishness.
- It symbolizes the burial of that old life, just as Jesus Himself was buried after His death.
- It symbolizes our resurrection to a whole new life, just as Jesus was resurrected, and, in our new life, Jesus lives in us by His Spirit.
- It demonstrates our faith in what Jesus has done for us, what He is doing for us right now each day, and what He will do for us in the great Resurrection day.

What does the Lord's Supper (communion) teach us?

BEFORE THE LAST SUPPER, JESUS LEFT US THE EXAMPLE OF FOOT-WASHING:

"So when He had washed their feet, taken His garments, and sat down again, He said to them, 'Do you know what I have done to you? You call Me Teacher and Lord, and you say well, for so I am. If I then, your Lord and Teacher, have washed your feet, you also ought to wash one another's feet. For I have given you an example, that you should do as I have done to you.' " —John 13:12–15.

THE RECORD OF THE ORIGINAL LORD'S SUPPER:

"And as they were eating, Jesus took bread, blessed and broke it, and gave it to the disciples and said, 'Take, eat; this is My body.'

"Then He took the cup, and gave thanks, and gave it to them, saying, 'Drink from it, all of you. For this is My blood of the new covenant, which is shed for many for the remission of sins.' " —Matthew 26:25–28.

JESUS ESTABLISHED THE SYMBOL OF THE LORD'S SUPPER:

"For I received from the Lord that which I also delivered to you: that the Lord Jesus on the same night in which He was betrayed took bread; and when He had given thanks, He broke it and said, 'Take, eat; this is My body which is broken for you; do this in remembrance of Me.' In the same manner He also took the cup after supper, saying, 'This cup is the new covenant in My blood. This do, as often as you drink it, in remembrance of Me. For as often as you eat this bread and drink this cup, you proclaim the Lord's death till He comes. Therefore whoever eats this bread or drinks this cup of the Lord in an unworthy manner will be guilty of the body and blood of the Lord. But let a man examine himself, and so let him eat of the bread and drink of the cup. For he who eats and drinks in an unworthy manner eats and drinks judgment to himself, not discerning the Lord's body. For this reason many are weak and sick among you, and many sleep.' " —1 Corinthians 11:23–30.

THE COMMUNION SERVICE OF BREAD AND WINE:

"The cup of blessing which we bless, is it not the communion of the blood of Christ? The bread which we break, is it not the communion of the body of Christ? For we, though many, are one bread and one body; for we all partake of that one bread." —1 Corinthians 10:16, 17.

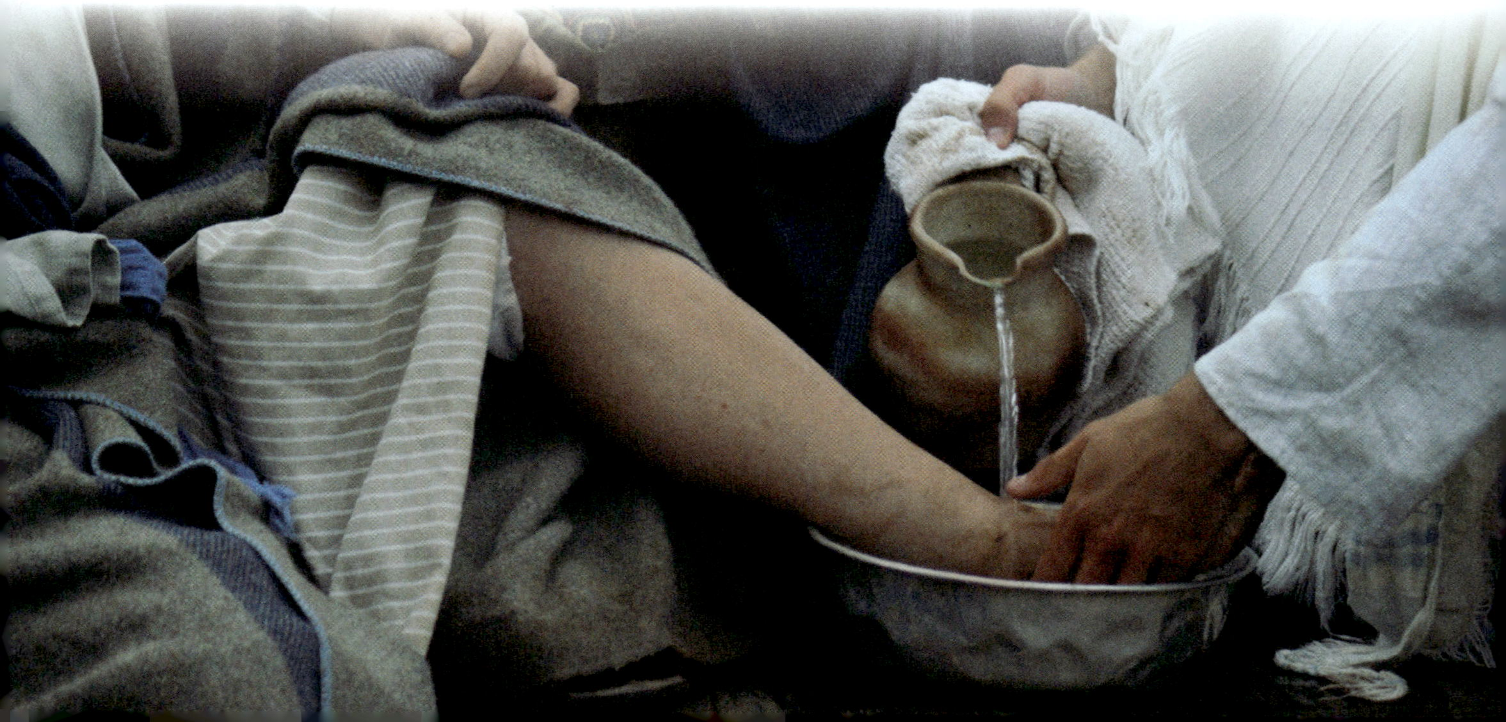

CHAPTER 15

SPIRITUAL GIFTS AND CHRISTIAN SERVICE

The Bible is clear that Jesus is the Head of His Church—and that the Church is His Body here on earth.

Just as a human body has many parts, each of which is designed to carry out a task or maybe a set of tasks, God's Church is composed of many members, each of whom God intends should carry out a task or perhaps more than just one. To perform those tasks, Christ gives each church member special spiritual gifts so they can carry out their assignments for Him efficiently and easily.

What topic should we especially know about?

"Now concerning spiritual gifts, brethren, I do not want you to be ignorant." —1 Corinthians 12:1.

"There are diversities of gifts, but the same Spirit. There are differences of ministries, but the same Lord. And there are diversities of activities, but it is the same God who works all in all. But the manifestation of the Spirit is given to each one for the profit of all. —1 Corinthians 12:4–7.

"But to each one of us grace was given according to the measure of Christ's gift. Therefore He says: 'When He ascended on high He led captivity captive, and gave gifts to men.'" —Ephesians 4:7, 8.

What spiritual gifts does the Bible identify?

"For to one is given the WORD OF WISDOM through the Spirit, to another the WORD OF KNOWLEDGE through the same Spirit, to another FAITH by the same Spirit, to another GIFTS OF HEALINGS by the same Spirit, to another the WORKING OF MIRACLES, to another PROPHECY, to another DISCERNING OF SPIRITS, to another DIFFERENT KINDS OF TONGUES, to another the INTERPRETATION OF TONGUES. But one and the same Spirit works all these things, distributing to each one individually as He wills." —1 Corinthians 12:8–11. emphasis supplied.

"And God has appointed these in the church: first APOSTLES, second PROPHETS, third TEACHERS, after that MIRACLES, then gifts of HEALINGS,

HELPS, ADMINISTRATIONS, VARIETIES OF TONGUES." —1 Corinthians 12:28, emphasis supplied.

"And He Himself gave some to be APOSTLES, some PROPHETS, some EVANGELISTS, and some PASTORS and TEACHERS," —Ephesians 4:11, emphasis supplied.

Let's Summarize

- The Word of Wisdom
- The Word of Knowledge
- Faith
- Healing
- Miracles
- Prophecy/Prophets
- Tongues
- Interpretation of Tongues
- Apostles
- Evangelists
- Pastors
- Teachers

What is the purpose of spiritual gifts?

"For the equipping of the saints for the work of ministry, for the edifying of the body of Christ, till we all come to the unity of the faith and of the knowledge of the Son of God, to a perfect man, to the measure of the stature of the fullness of Christ." —Ephesians 4:12, 13.

NOTE: Clearly, the main reason for God giving His church members spiritual gifts is "for the equipping of the saints for the work of ministry."

It is not for the saints to only *support* the work of the ministers, apostles, evangelists, and teachers. Though these too are needed spiritual gifts, God's intent is that EVERY MEMBER be a minister.

God's Church is not made up of a few "professionals" who do the work of the Church while everyone else stays on the sidelines as spectators.

If you are a church member, God has given you spiritual gifts that are indispensably needed. The task God gives you is as important as that of any pastor or evangelist.

Do we choose our own spiritual gifts? Or does God assign them?

"But one and the same Spirit works all these things, distributing to each one individually as He wills." —1 Corinthians 12:11.

The Holy Spirit distributes spiritual gifts as HE wills, or chooses—not as we choose or wish.

What if we are not happy with the gift God has given us?

"If the foot should say, 'Because I am not a hand, I am not of the body,' is it therefore not of the body? And if the ear should say, 'Because I am not an eye, I am not of the body,' is it therefore not of the body? If the whole body were an eye, where would be the hearing? If the whole were hearing, where would be the smelling? But now God has set the members, each one of them, in the body just as He pleased. And if they were all one member, where would the body be? But now indeed there are many members, yet one body. And the eye cannot say to the hand, 'I have no need of you'; nor again the head to the feet, 'I have no need of you.' No, much rather, those members of the body which seem to be weaker are necessary. And those members of the body which we think to be less honorable, on these we bestow greater honor; and our unpresentable parts have greater modesty, but our presentable parts have no need. But God composed the body, having given greater honor to that part which lacks it, that there should be no schism in the body, but that the members should have the same care for one another. And if one member suffers, all the members suffer with it; or if one member is honored, all the members rejoice with it." —1 Corinthians 12:15–26.

Some Thought Questions About Spiritual Gifts

- Is there a difference between talents and spiritual gifts?
- Is the spiritual gift of a pastor or evangelist more important than the gift of helps or faith?
- How do I discover my own spiritual gift or gifts?
- Will using my spiritual gift bring satisfaction and a sense of reward?
- We hear that every one of us should witness for Christ. Does that mean that I must preach or hold Bible studies or knock on doors? Or could my most effective way to witness be in exercising my Spirit-assigned spiritual gifts?
- Do you think that if—after I'm given my spiritual gift(s), I leave the Church Body—that I still retain my gift(s)? Why—or why not?

Will spiritual gifts last forever?

"Love never fails. But whether there are prophecies, they will fail; whether there are tongues, they will cease; whether there is knowledge, it will vanish away. For we know in part and we prophesy in part. But when that which is perfect has come, then that which is in part will be done away." —1 Corinthians 13:8–10.

CHAPTER 16

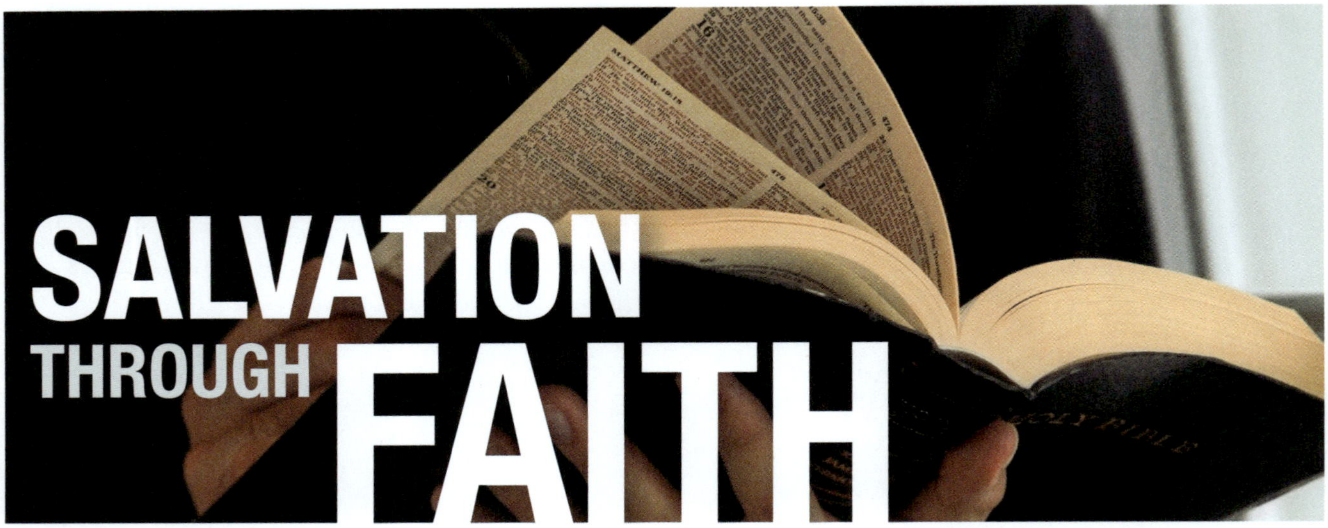

SALVATION THROUGH FAITH

In the Bible, we learn that God deals with everything necessary to remove sin from us: At the cross, He removed its penalty. By His indwelling Spirit, He removes its power—its hold over us. When He takes His faithful followers to heaven after the Second Coming, He removes from us—and from His entire universe—the very presence of sin.

Our salvation would not be complete without deliverance from all three: sin's PENALTY, its POWER, and its PRESENCE.

How did Jesus remove sin's penalty from us at the Cross?

"All have sinned and fall short of the glory of God." —Romans 3:23.

"For the wages of sin is death." —Romans 6:23.

"Therefore, just as through one man sin entered the world, and death through sin, and thus death spread to all men, because all sinned. ... Therefore, as through one man's offense judgment came to all men, resulting in condemnation, even so through one Man's righteous act the free gift came to all men, resulting in justification of life. For as by one man's disobedience many were made sinners, so also by one Man's obedience many will be made righteous." —Romans 5:12, 18, 19.

Let's Summarize:

1. We have all sinned.
2. The wages of sin is death.
3. The sin of one man (Adam) passed on to the entire human race, making us all sinners and putting us all under condemnation.
4. The righteousness of one Man (Jesus) passed also on to the entire human race, making us all righteous and putting us all under justification.
5. So we have two Adams. Adam Number One—and Adam Number Two. "And so it is written, 'The first man Adam [Adam, of Eden] became a living being.' The last Adam [Jesus] became a life-giving spirit." —1 Corinthians 15:45.

6. Biologically, we all trace our physical lives back to Adam in Eden. But spiritually, we can trace our lives back to the perfect life of Jesus.
7. In fact, God has already placed us in Jesus: "But of Him [God the Father] you are IN Christ Jesus." —1 Corinthians 1:30, emphasis supplied.
8. So unless we actively choose not to remain in Jesus—to reject His substitutionary life for ours—we are justified, no longer under condemnation, as perfect in God's sight as if we had never sinned.

In the words of a gifted spiritual author:

> "Christ was treated as we deserve, that we might be treated as He deserves. He was condemned for our sins, in which He had no share, that we might be justified by His righteousness, in which we had no share. He suffered the death which was ours, that we might receive the life which was His." —Ellen White, *The Desire of Ages*, p. 25.

What an exchange!

How does Jesus remove sin's power from us?

SO CLEARLY, IF WE WERE JUSTIFIED AT THE CROSS, WE ARE NO LONGER UNDER THE CONDEMNATION OF THE LAW:

"Therefore, having been justified by faith, we have peace with God through our Lord Jesus Christ." —Romans 5:1.

"There is therefore now no condemnation to those who are in Christ Jesus." —Romans 8:1.

BUT EVEN THOUGH GOD HAS DECISIVELY DEALT WITH SIN'S PENALTY AT THE CROSS, WHAT ABOUT THE POWER OF SIN—THE HOLD IT HAS IN OUR HABITS AND THOUGHTS AND BEHAVIORS?

"Moreover the law entered that the offense might abound. But where sin abounded, grace abounded much more, so that as sin reigned in death, even so grace might reign through righteousness to eternal life through Jesus Christ our Lord. … What shall we say then? Shall we continue in sin that grace may abound? Certainly not! How shall we who died to sin live any longer in it? Or do you not know that as many of us as were baptized into Christ Jesus were baptized into His death? Therefore we were buried with Him through baptism into death, that just as Christ was raised from the dead by the glory of the Father, even so we also should walk in newness of life." —Romans 5:20, 21; 6:1–4.

SO BEING SAVED FROM SIN'S PENALTY IS NOT A LICENSE TO "CONTINUE IN SIN"! BUT HOW DO WE ESCAPE SIN'S POWER?

"I have been crucified with Christ; it is no longer I who live, but Christ lives in me; and the life which I now live in the flesh I live by faith in the Son of God, who loved me and gave Himself for me." —Galatians 2:20.

The Bible presents twin themes: "you in Christ" and "Christ in you." In Christ, I receive justification and am no longer condemned. But with Christ in me, He lives out His perfect life in me, breaking its power in my life day by day, hour by hour. This is called sanctification. My part in both of these is faith—trust in what Jesus has done for me at the cross, and what He does for me in the here and now.

Finally, how does Jesus remove sin's very presence from my life?

Let's Begin with a home made Parable:

Three couch potatoes sprawled across the living room furniture one evening in front of the TV, when their favorite programs were suddenly interrupted by that laundry detergent commercial starring the Mud Puddle Kid.

Up on the screen, a weary mother looked blissfully grateful for the box of Mud-B-Gone detergent she hugged tightly in her arms, as—out in the street in front of the house—her young son stomped gleefully through the mud puddles in his freshly laundered pants.

"Would you look at that?" remarked Couch Potato #1. "That kid has messed up his spanking-clean clothes with that yucky mud. Good thing his mom has that detergent."

"Well, maybe," added Couch Potato #2, "but what good does it do for her to wash his clothes, if all he does is run right back out and stomp through the puddles again? What this kid needs is for somebody to make it so that he does not even want to stomp in puddles again."

Up on the TV screen, the Mud Puddle Kid continued to splatter himself in muddy goo, as Couch Potato #3 put in his two cents' worth. "It's one thing to clean up the kid when he gets muddy," he said. "And it's another to fix it so he does not even want to get muddy again. But what would really solve everything is if somebody could take the mud puddles themselves away. Now that would truly be good news!"

Well, it pains me to say it, but the Three Couch Potatoes got into such an argument over who had the right solution—over what was really Good News—that they ended up out in the street in front of their own house, each slinging mud at the others.

Sad to say, Christians sometimes get into the same kind of argument about the Good News of salvation. Some say that when we get all covered with the mud of sin, we need God to forgive us and clean us up. Others say that this does not do much good unless somehow, God can do something about our desire to keep sinning. And finally, some say that we can never be fully saved from sin until God takes sin itself away.

The complete Good News? God delivers us from sin's penalty, power, and presence.

In the previous sections of this chapter, we took a look at those first two—Justification and Sanctification. Now let's take a minute to consider Glorification. If Justification delivers us from sin's penalty, and Sanctification delivers us from sin's power, God's Plan of Salvation will not be completed until Glorification delivers us from sin's very presence.

Because of the cross, our salvation is assured. We are justified by faith in Christ's sacrifice. Because of Christ's dwelling in us through the Spirit, the power of sin—its hold over us—is steadily broken through our entire life. But God's plan does not include our living forever in the presence of sin and temptation. Sin itself will ultimately be destroyed.

At the Second Coming, we are glorified. We receive new minds and bodies with no sin whatever in our natures. And at the end of the thousand years in heaven described in Revelation 20, God destroys sin itself and its author, Satan. The earth is purified of every trace of sin.

Our glorified minds will never again feel the pull of sin—never again know a single temptation. Our glorified bodies will bear not a single evidence of sin—no sickness, no pain, no aging, no fatigue, no scars or wounds or deformities. Our glorified hearts will never feel grief or sadness or heartbreak or loss. We'll never again shed a solitary tear.

> "O Death, where is your sting? O Hades, where is your victory? The sting of death is sin."—1 Corinthians 15:55, 56. With sin gone at the end, so will be its result: death.

> "And God will wipe away every tear from their eyes; there shall be no more death, nor sorrow, nor crying. There shall be no more pain, for the former things have passed away." —Revelation 21:4.

CHAPTER 17

THE MINISTRY OF ANGELS

Angels are countless in number, the Bible says. They surround God's throne, worship Him constantly, carry out His missions and tasks, work with Him to minister to the human beings in this sinful world, and they excel in strength and power.

Originally, before sin, they were perfect and sinless, but when sin arose in the heart of heaven's chief angel, Lucifer, a third of the angels followed him into rebellion. Today, the good angels and evil angels war unseen over you and me.

What is the relationship between angels and human beings?

HUMANS ARE CREATED JUST A LITTLE LOWER THAN THE ANGELS:

"What is man that You are mindful of him, and the son of man that You visit him? For You have made him a little lower than the angels, and You have crowned him with glory and honor." —Psalm 8:4, 5.

ANGELS ARE SENT TO MINISTER TO US:

"Are they not all ministering spirits sent forth to minister for those who will inherit salvation?" —Hebrews 1:14.

ANGELS DESIRE TO LOOK INTO AND UNDERSTAND THE PLAN OF SALVATION:

"Those who have preached the gospel to you by the Holy Spirit sent from heaven—things which angels desire to look into." —1 Peter 1:12.

ANGELS REJOICE WHEN WE REPENT:

"Likewise, I say to you, there is joy in the presence of the angels of God over one sinner who repents." —Luke 15:10.

ANGELS PROTECT US:

"Because you have made the Lord, who is my refuge, even the Most High, your dwelling place, no evil shall befall you, nor shall any plague come near your dwelling; for He shall give His angels charge over you, to keep you in all your ways. In their hands they shall bear you up, lest you dash your foot against a stone." —Psalm 91:9–12.

"The angel of the Lord encamps all around those who fear Him, and delivers them." —Psalm 34:7.

ANGELS PROTECT CHILDREN:

"Take heed that you do not despise one of these little ones, for I say to you that in heaven their angels always see the face of My Father who is in heaven." —Matthew 18:10.

What facts does the Bible share with us about angels?

ONE DESCRIPTION OF THEIR NUMBER:

"Then I looked, and I heard the voice of many angels around the throne, the living creatures, and the elders; and the number of them was ten thousand times ten thousand, and thousands of thousands." —Revelation 5:11.

AND ANOTHER . . . :

"But you have come to Mount Zion and to the city of the living God, the heavenly Jerusalem, to an innumerable company of angels." —Hebrews 12:22.

THEY EXCEL IN STRENGTH:

"Bless the Lord, you His angels, who excel in strength, who do His word, heeding the voice of His word." —Psalm 103:20.

ANGELS MAY TAKE HUMAN FORM:

"Do not forget to entertain strangers, for by so doing some have unwittingly entertained angels." —Hebrews 13:2.

How does the Bible describe the ministry of angels through history?

ANGELS GUARDED EDEN AFTER ADAM AND EVE FELL INTO SIN:

"Then the Lord God said, 'Behold, the man has become like one of Us, to know good and evil. And now, lest he put out his hand and take also of the tree of life, and eat, and live forever'—therefore the Lord God sent him out of the garden of Eden to till the ground from which he was taken. So He drove out the man; and He placed cherubim [cherubim are one of the orders of angels—see box on next page] at the east of the garden of Eden, and a flaming sword which turned every way, to guard the way to the tree of life." —Genesis 3:22–24.

AN ANGEL ROLLED AWAY THE STONE FROM CHRIST'S TOMB:

"And behold, there was a great earthquake; for an angel of the Lord descended from heaven, and came and rolled back the stone from the door, and sat on it. His countenance was like lightning, and his clothing as white as snow." —Matthew 28:2, 3.

ONE OR MORE ANGELS SAVED THE THREE HEBREW WORTHIES IN NEBUCHADNEZZAR'S FURNACE:

" 'Look!' he answered, 'I see four men loose, walking in the midst of the fire; and they are not hurt, and the form of the fourth is like the Son of God.' Then Nebuchadnezzar went near the mouth of the burning fiery furnace and spoke, saying, 'Shadrach, Meshach, and Abed-Nego, servants of the Most High God, come out, and come here.' Then Shadrach, Meshach, and Abed-Nego came from the midst of the fire. And the satraps, administrators, governors, and the king's counselors gathered together, and they saw these men on whose bodies the fire had no power; the hair of their head was not singed nor were their garments affected, and the smell of fire was not on them. Nebuchadnezzar spoke, saying, 'Blessed be the God of Shadrach, Meshach, and Abed-Nego, who sent His Angel and delivered His servants who trusted in Him, and they have frustrated the king's word, and yielded their bodies, that they should not serve nor worship any god except their own God!' " —Daniel 3:25–28.

AN ANGEL DELIVERED THE APOSTLES FROM PRISON:

"But at night an angel of the Lord opened the prison doors and brought them out." —Acts 5:19.

AN ANGEL MINISTERED TO JESUS AFTER HIS WILDERNESS TEMPTATIONS:

"Then the devil left Him, and behold, angels came and ministered to Him." —Matthew 4:11.

AN ANGEL MINISTERED TO JESUS DURING HIS GETHSEMANE PRAYER:

"Then an angel appeared to Him from heaven, strengthening Him." —Luke 22:43.

COUNTLESS ANGELS WILL BE PRESENT AT THE JUDGMENT:

"A fiery stream issued and came forth from before Him. A thousand thousands ministered to Him; ten thousand times ten thousand stood before Him. The court was seated, and the books were opened." —Daniel 7:10.

The Orders of Heaven's Angels

The Bible speaks of at least three orders or types of angels:

- Cherubim: Genesis 3:24—posted to guard the entrance to Eden after the fall of man.
- Seraphim: Isaiah 6:2, 6—six-winged angels who stand in God's immediate presence.
- Archangel: 1 Thessalonians 4:16; Jude 9—the name for the chief over all angels—Jesus Christ Himself, also called Michael.

What does the Bible say about evil angels?

"For … God did not spare the angels who sinned, but cast them down to hell [Greek: "A place of darkness" … considered to be this world] and delivered them into chains of darkness, to be reserved for judgment." —2 Peter 2:4.

DRAGON = SATAN; ONE-THIRD OF HEAVEN'S ANGELS REBELLED WITH HIM:

"And another sign appeared in heaven: behold, a great, fiery red dragon having seven heads and ten horns, and seven diadems on his heads. His tail drew a third of the stars of heaven and threw them to the earth." —Revelation 12:3, 4.

"For we do not wrestle against flesh and blood, but against principalities, against powers, against the rulers of the darkness of this age, against spiritual hosts of wickedness [evil angels] in the heavenly places." —Ephesians 6:12.

BEWARE OF THE DEVIL AND HIS ANGELS NEAR THE END OF TIME:

"For the devil has come down to you, having great wrath, because he knows that he has a short time." —Revelation 12:12.

THE FATE OF EVIL ANGELS:

"Then He will also say to those on the left hand, 'Depart from Me, you cursed, into the everlasting fire prepared for the devil and his angels.' " —Matthew 25:41.

"For behold, the day is coming, burning like an oven, and all the proud, yes, all who do wickedly will be stubble. And the day which is coming shall burn them up,' says the Lord of hosts." —Malachi 4:1.

CHAPTER 18

GOD'S PLAN FOR FINANCIAL SECURITY

God is the owner of everything. He owns His entire universe. He owns this earth—and everything on it. All its gold and silver, all its wealth, and every living thing. We human beings think we own things: parcels of land, buildings, cars, homes, bank accounts, savings and investments. But everything we have is from God. And when it comes to all of God's created "things" on earth, He wants to team up with us as our business partner—He as the owner, and we as His managers—sometimes called stewards. Let's explore what the Bible says on this.

Does God really own everything?

"For every beast of the forest is Mine, and the cattle on a thousand hills. I know all the birds of the mountains, and the wild beasts of the field are Mine. If I were hungry, I would not tell you; for the world is Mine, and all its fullness.' —Psalm 50:10–12.

" 'The silver is Mine, and the gold is Mine,' says the Lord of hosts." —Haggai 2:8.

"The earth is the Lord's, and all its fullness, the world and those who dwell therein." —Psalm 24:1.

LIFE, BREATH, AND ALL THINGS:

"Nor is He worshiped with men's hands, as though He needed anything, since He gives to all life, breath, and all things." —Acts 17:25.

What do we have that comes from God?

"For all that is in heaven and in earth is Yours; Yours is the kingdom, O Lord, and You are exalted as head over all. Both riches and honor come from You." —1 Chronicles 29:11, 12.

"Beware that you do not forget the Lord your God by not keeping His commandments, His judgments, and His statutes which I command you today, lest—when you have eaten and are full, and have built beautiful houses and dwell in them; and when your herds and your flocks multiply, and your silver and your gold are multiplied, and all that you have is multiplied; when your heart is lifted up, and you forget the Lord your God who brought you out of the land of Egypt, from the house of bondage; who led you through that great and terrible wilderness, in which were fiery serpents and scorpions and thirsty land where there was no water; who brought water for you out of the flinty rock; who fed you in the wilderness with manna, which your fathers did not know, that He might humble you and that He might test you, to do you good in the end—then you say in your heart, 'My power and the might of my hand have gained me this wealth.' And you shall remember the Lord your God, for IT IS HE WHO GIVES YOU POWER TO GET WEALTH." —Deuteronomy 8:11–18, emphasis supplied.

How Does One Become Wealthy—Or at Least Financially Secure?

Most would say:

- Work hard.
- Save regularly.
- Start a business.
- Receive an inheritance.
- Work long hours at an hourly or salaried job.
- Become good at selling something.

All of these can produce income, even to the point of wealth. But who gives you the power to get wealth? The creativity? The originality and initiative and innovative thoughts? The energy? The stamina? All of this comes from God, even if we don't acknowledge it.

In partnership with God, He keeps just 10 percent; we keep 90 percent

THE GREATEST FINANCIAL SECURITY RESULTS FROM PARTNERING WITH GOD:

"And all the tithe of the land, whether of the seed of the land or of the fruit of the tree, is the Lord's. It is holy to the Lord. If a man wants at all to redeem any of his tithes, he shall add one-fifth to it. And concerning the tithe of the herd or the flock, of whatever passes under the rod, the tenth one shall be holy to the Lord." —Leviticus 27:30–32.

" 'Yet from the days of your fathers you have gone away from My ordinances and have not kept them. Return to Me, and I will return to you,' says the Lord of hosts. But you said, 'In what way shall we return?' Will a man rob God? Yet you have robbed Me! But you say, 'In what way have we robbed You?' In tithes and offerings. You are cursed with a curse, for you have robbed Me, even this whole nation. Bring all the tithes into the storehouse, that there may be food in My house, and try Me now in this, says the Lord of hosts, if I will not open for you the windows of heaven and pour out for you such blessing that there will not be room enough to receive it." —Malachi 3:7–10.

"Woe to you, scribes and Pharisees, hypocrites! For you pay tithe of mint and anise and cummin, and have neglected the weightier matters of the law: justice and mercy and faith. These you ought to have done, without leaving the others undone." —Matthew 23:23.

What is the tithe to be used for?

THE LEVITES WERE THE MINISTERS OF THE OLD TESTAMENT:

"Behold, I have given the children of Levi all the tithes in Israel as an inheritance in return for the work which they perform, the work of the tabernacle of meeting." —Numbers 18:21.

THE SAME PRINCIPLE IS SEEN IN THE NEW TESTAMENT:

"Do you not know that those who minister the holy things eat of the things of the temple, and those who serve at the altar partake of the offerings of the altar? Even so the Lord has commanded that those who preach the gospel should live from the gospel." —1 Corinthians 9:13, 14.

What is God's promise if we put Him first?

TO REPEAT THE GREAT TITHING PROMISE:

" 'Bring all the tithes into the storehouse, that there may be food in My house, and try Me now in this,' says the Lord of hosts, 'If I will not open for you the windows of heaven and pour out for you such blessing that there will not be room enough to receive it." —Malachi 3:10.

"Therefore do not worry, saying, 'What shall we eat?' or 'What shall we drink?' or 'What shall we wear?' For after all these things the Gentiles seek. For your heavenly Father knows that you need all these things. But seek first the kingdom of God and His righteousness, and all these things shall be added to you. Therefore do not worry about tomorrow, for tomorrow will worry about its own things. Sufficient for the day is its own trouble." —Matthew 6:31–34.

"I have been young, and now am old; yet I have not seen the righteous forsaken, nor his descendants begging bread." —Psalm 37:25.

"But this I say: He who sows sparingly will also reap sparingly, and he who sows bountifully will also reap bountifully. So let each one give as he purposes in his heart, not grudgingly or of necessity; for God loves a cheerful giver." —2 Corinthians 9:6, 7.

Does Partnering with God Make Good Sense?

- If we tithe, He pours out such a blessing we won't have room enough to receive it.
- No one who has partnered with God has had to go begging in order to eat.
- He keeps just 10 percent; we keep 90 percent.
- He promises that if we put Him first, He WILL take care of our food, clothing, and other needs.

Imagine the worry saved if we realize that God makes Himself responsible for our material and financial needs!

CHAPTER 19

THE BLESSING OF TOTAL HEALTH

Even in a world filled with illness and disease—with bacteria and viruses and other unfriendly microbes—God wants us to be healthy. Even in a world where pollution afflicts our air and water, and where our food supply is often less than ideal, God wants us to be healthy.

The God who made our human bodies knows how they can be kept healthy. He has shared laws and principles of health with us, which, if followed, result in abundant health.

What is God's will concerning our health?

"Beloved, I pray that you may prosper in all things and be in health, just as your soul prospers." —3 John 2.

"If you diligently heed the voice of the Lord your God and do what is right in His sight, give ear to His commandments and keep all His statutes, I will put none of the diseases on you which I have brought on the Egyptians. For I am the Lord who heals you." —Exodus 15:26.

"Therefore, whether you eat or drink, or whatever you do, do all to the glory of God." —1 Corinthians 10:31.

What does God consider our bodies to be?

"Do you not know that you are the temple of God and that the Spirit of God dwells in you? If anyone defiles the temple of God, God will destroy him. For the temple of God is holy, which temple you are." —1 Corinthians 3:16, 17.

"Or do you not know that your body is the temple of the Holy Spirit who is in you, whom you have from God, and you are not your own? For you were bought at a price; therefore glorify God in your body and in your spirit, which are God's." —1 Corinthians 6:19, 20.

Building Up God's Temple—Or Tearing It Down?

Which ways do we <u>build up</u> our body temples?

- ☐ Eating healthfully
- ☐ Going without enough sleep
- ☐ Eating junk and fast food
- ☐ Smoking, drinking, taking recreational drugs
- ☐ Sitting all day and staying sedentary
- ☐ Drinking lots of coffee and energy drinks
- ☐ Casting our cares and worries on God
- ☐ Breathing deeply as often as possible
- ☐ Exercising regularly
- ☐ Staying connected with God through prayer and the study of His Word
- ☐ Letting negative emotions control us: anger, resentment, unforgiveness, fear, guilt

What is the ideal diet for good health?

MAN'S ORIGINAL DIET:

"And God said, 'See, I have given you every herb that yields seed which is on the face of all the earth, and every tree whose fruit yields seed; to you it shall be for food.'" —Genesis 1:29.

CLEAN AND UNCLEAN ANIMALS ENTERED THE ARK:

"You shall take with you seven each of every clean animal, a male and his female; two each of animals that are unclean, a male and his female." —Genesis 7:2.

VEGETABLES ADDED AFTER MANKIND FELL IN EDEN:

"Cursed is the ground for your sake; in toil you shall eat of it all the days of your life. Both thorns and thistles it shall bring forth for you, and you shall eat the herb of the field." —Genesis 3:17, 18.

FLESH FOOD PERMITTED AFTER THE FLOOD:

"And the fear of you and the dread of you shall be on every beast of the earth, on every bird of the air, on all that move on the earth, and on all the fish of the sea. They are given into your hand. Every moving thing that lives shall be food for you. I have given you all things, even as the green herbs." —Genesis 9:2, 3.

CLEAN AND UNCLEAN FLESH FOODS DEFINED: See Leviticus 11:1–31.

What warnings does the Bible give concerning use of alcohol?

"Wine is a mocker, strong drink is a brawler, and whoever is led astray by it is not wise." —Proverbs 20:1.

"Now therefore, please be careful not to drink wine or similar drink, and not to eat anything unclean." —Judges 13:4.

"Who has woe? Who has sorrow? Who has contentions? Who has complaints? Who has wounds without cause? Who has redness of eyes? Those who linger long at the wine, those who go in search of mixed wine. Do not look on the wine when it is red, when it sparkles in the cup, when it swirls around smoothly; at the last it bites like a serpent, and stings like a viper." —Proverbs 23:29–32.

"Neither fornicators, nor idolaters, nor adulterers, nor homosexuals, nor sodomites, nor thieves, nor covetous, nor drunkards, nor revilers, nor extortioners will inherit the kingdom of God." —1 Corinthians 6:9, 10.

Eight Proven Rules for Excellent Health

N = Nutrition

E = Exercise

W = Water

S = Sunlight

T = Temperance

A = Air

R = Rest

T = Trust in Divine Power

NEWSTART is an acronym developed by Weimar Institute, Weimar, California.

It's a Choice—Just a Choice!

Changing health habits may seem intimidating—almost impossible. But not really!

Changing ANY habit begins with a simple choice. Instead of trying to overhaul your complete diet overnight, begin with one or two changes and focus on them for a week or two. Then add some other changes.

Same thing with other health habits. Start walking—just a short distance per day, then keep adding on.

Keep a water bottle nearby and drink more during the day. Practice breathing deeply several times a day. Work on getting more sleep. Little choices lead to major habit changes!

CHAPTER 20

WHAT HAPPENS WHEN WE DIE?

One of the greatest of life's mysteries is what happens when life ends—when we die. Where do we go? What becomes of us? Happily, the Bible is clear in answering these questions.

As we study the Word, we find how each of us is put together—about body, soul, and spirit. We find out where our loved ones are who have passed on—and where we too will be when we finally breathe our last. But we also learn about the beautiful life that awaits us after this one. So let's open the Book and learn together!

Do we have a soul?

"And the Lord God formed man of the dust of the ground, and breathed into his nostrils the breath of life; and man became a living being. [King James: "soul"]" —Genesis 2:7.

Dust + Breath of life = Living being (soul). So we do not HAVE souls—we ARE souls!

AT DEATH, THE PROCESS IS REVERSED:

"Then the dust will return to the earth as it was, and the spirit will return to God who gave it." —Ecclesiastes 12:7.

SO AT DEATH, THERE IS NO CONSCIOUS "SOUL" THAT LIVES ON. THE BREATH OF LIFE, OR SPIRIT, SIMPLY RETURNS TO GOD WHO GAVE IT.

What does the Bible call death?

"These things He said, and after that He said to them, 'Our friend Lazarus sleeps, but I go that I may wake him up.' Then His disciples said, 'Lord, if he sleeps he will get well.' However, Jesus spoke of his death, but they thought that He was speaking about taking rest in sleep. Then Jesus said to them plainly, 'Lazarus is dead.' " —John 11:11–14.

"Consider and hear me, O Lord my God; enlighten my eyes, lest I sleep the sleep of death." —Psalm 13:3.

"And many of those who sleep in the dust of the earth shall awake, some to everlasting life, some to shame and everlasting contempt." —Daniel 12:2.

Are the dead conscious and aware?

SPEAKING OF THE DEAD:

"His sons come to honor, and he does not know it; they are brought low, and he does not perceive it." —Job 14:21.

NO ONE CAN LAY PLANS AFTER DEATH:

"Do not put your trust in princes, nor in a son of man, in whom there is no help. His spirit departs, he returns to his earth; in that very day his plans perish." —Psalm 146:3, 4.

THE DEAD KNOW NOTHING:

"For the living know that they will die; but the dead know nothing, and they have no more reward, for the memory of them is forgotten. Also their love, their hatred, and their envy have now perished; nevermore will they have a share in anything done under the sun." —Ecclesiastes 9:5, 6.

DEAD REMEMBER NOTHING AND CAN'T GIVE THANKS:

"For in death there is no remembrance of You; in the grave who will give You thanks?" —Psalm 6:5.

DEAD DO NOT PRAISE GOD:

"The dead do not praise the Lord, nor any who go down into silence." —Psalm 115:17.

AGAIN, THE DEAD DO NOT PRAISE GOD:

"What profit is there in my blood, when I go down to the pit? Will the dust praise You? Will it declare Your truth?" —Psalm 30:9.

ARE THEY BIBLICAL?

In light of the Bible's teaching, what do you think? What are the chances these are biblical?

- ☐ Ghosts
- ☐ Zombies
- ☐ Poltergeists
- ☐ Haunted houses
- ☐ The "Walking Dead"
- ☐ Werewolves
- ☐ Spirits of the dead
- ☐ Reincarnated beings
- ☐ Shape-shifters
- ☐ Aliens

Do the dead go to heaven or hell at death?

"Yet shall he be brought to the grave, and shall remain in the tomb." —Job 21:32, KJV.

"As the cloud disappears and vanishes away, so he who goes down to the grave does not come up. He shall never return to his house, nor shall his place know him anymore." —Job 7:9, 10.

DEAD ARE IN THE GRAVE TILL THE RESURRECTION DAY:

"Do not marvel at this; for the hour is coming in which all who are in the graves will hear His voice and come forth—those who have done good, to the resurrection of life, and those who have done evil, to the resurrection of condemnation." —John 5:28, 29.

DAVID DID NOT GO TO HEAVEN AT DEATH:

"Men and brethren, let me speak freely to you of the patriarch David, that he is both dead and buried, and his tomb is with us to this day. Therefore, being a prophet, and knowing that God had sworn with an oath to him that of the fruit of his body, according to the flesh, He would raise up the Christ to sit on his throne, he, foreseeing this, spoke concerning the resurrection of the Christ, that His soul was not left in Hades, nor did His flesh see corruption. This Jesus God has raised up, of which we are all witnesses. Therefore being exalted to the right hand of God, and having received from the Father the promise of the Holy Spirit, He poured out this which you now see and hear. For David did not ascend into the heavens, but he says himself: 'The Lord said to my Lord, "Sit at My right hand, Till I make Your enemies Your footstool." ' " —Acts 2:29–35.

EVEN JESUS DID NOT GO DIRECTLY TO HEAVEN AT HIS RESURRECTION:

"Jesus said to her, 'Do not cling to Me, for I have not yet ascended to My Father.' " —John 20:17.

Are human beings immortal?

THE MAJORITY OF CHRISTIANS BELIEVE AND PREACH THAT WE HAVE IMMORTAL SOULS THAT SURVIVE DEATH. WHAT DOES THE BIBLE SAY?

HUMAN IMMORTALITY: THE DEVIL'S FIRST LIE:

"Then the serpent said to the woman, 'You will not surely die.' " —Genesis 3:4.

"Shall mortal man be more just than God? shall a man be more pure than his maker?" —Job 4:17, KJV.

"The soul who sins shall die." —Ezekiel 18:20.

ONLY GOD IS IMMORTAL:

"He who is the blessed and only Potentate, the King of kings and Lord of lords, who alone has immortality, dwelling in unapproachable light, whom no man has seen or can see, to whom be honor and everlasting power." —1 Timothy 6:15, 16.

"Now to the King eternal, immortal, invisible, to God who alone is wise, be honor and glory forever and ever. Amen." —1 Timothy 1:17.

THROUGH CHRIST, SOMEDAY IMMORTALITY WILL BE OURS:

"Our Savior Jesus Christ, who has abolished death and brought life and immortality to light through the gospel." —2 Timothy 1:10.

> "Death, be not proud, though some have called thee mighty and dreadful, for thou art not so; one short sleep past, we wake eternally and death shall be no more; death, thou shalt die."
> —John Donne

CHAPTER 21

SIGNS OF THE END OF TIME

When Jesus ascended back to heaven after His life, death, and resurrection here on earth, He promised to return again—and to take His faithful followers with Him to a new and perfect world forever.

Before leaving our world, He gave His followers a number of signs that would signal the nearness of His return. It is wise and encouraging for us to study those signs so that His coming will not come to us as a great surprise. Even the worsening of evil here on earth tells us that His return is near. Let us hear what the Word says:

What signs did Jesus give us that would signal the nearness of His return?

"Now as He sat on the Mount of Olives, the disciples came to Him privately, saying, 'Tell us, when will these things be? And what will be the sign of Your coming, and of the end of the age?' " —Matthew 24:3.

NOTE: In answer to this question from His disciples, Jesus spent most of the 24th chapter of Matthew in His reply.

But His reply included not only signs of His future Second Coming but also warnings of the much nearer destruction of the Temple, which would take place in A.D. 70, not long after His ascension back to heaven.

Therefore, it's important to do our best to determine which parts of Matthew 24 apply to the destruction of Jerusalem and the Temple—and which parts apply to the final years just before the Second Coming.

How does the Bible compare earth's final days with the days of Noah before the flood?

"But as the days of Noah were, so also will the coming of the Son of Man be. For as in the days before the flood, they were eating and drinking, marrying and giving in marriage, until the day that Noah entered the ark, and did not know until the flood came and took them all away, so also will the coming of the Son of Man be." —Matthew 24:37–39.

NOTE: The Bible isn't here condemning eating and drinking, marrying and giving in marriage. But before the Flood, nearly the entire world was focused on their own life pursuits, leaving God out of their lives.

Specific Signs in Matthew 24

- False christs
- Wars and rumors of wars
- Nation against nation; kingdom against kingdom
- Famines
- Pestilences (disease epidemics)
- Earthquakes
- Time of trouble
- False prophets
- Lawlessness abounding
- Love of many grows cold
- Gospel preached in all the world
- Sun darkened
- Moon not giving its light
- Stars falling from heaven

A careful study of Matthew 24 is required to determine which signs apply to the fall of Jerusalem and which to the days just prior to the Second Coming.

How else does the Bible describe earth's final days?

SCOFFERS WILL ARISE:

"Knowing this first: that scoffers will come in the last days, walking according to their own lusts, and saying, 'Where is the promise of His coming? For since the fathers fell asleep, all things continue as they were from the beginning of creation.' " —2 Peter 3:3, 4.

INTENSE EVIL:

"But know this, that in the last days perilous times will come: for men will be lovers of themselves, lovers of money, boasters, proud, blasphemers, disobedient to parents, unthankful, unholy, unloving, unforgiving, slanderers, without self-control, brutal, despisers of good, traitors, headstrong, haughty, lovers of pleasure rather than lovers of God, having a form of godliness but denying its power. And from such people turn away!" —2 Timothy 3:1–5.

Signs in the Sun, Moon, and Stars

In the box across the page, Matthew 24 lists signs in the sun, moon, and stars.

Many students of Bible prophecy believe these signs were fulfilled as follows:

- May 19, 1780—The sun refused to shine across much of New England.
- May 19, 1780—That same evening, the moon appeared as blood red.
- November 13, 1833—The greatest meteor shower of modern times took place, visible all across the eastern United States.

Other Bible students believe that while those signs were indeed impressive, others even more dramatic and widespread may yet take place before the end of time and the return of Jesus.

Perhaps the best approach when it comes to Bible signs of the end is to note well what has already occurred but to keep an open and alert mind in case God should choose to rivet the attention of a new and later generation on the nearness of Christ's return.

How does the Bible describe the harvest of good and evil prior to the second coming?

THE PARABLE OF THE WHEAT AND THE TARES (WEEDS):

"Another parable He put forth to them, saying: 'The kingdom of heaven is like a man who sowed good seed in his field; but while men slept, his enemy came and sowed tares among the wheat and went his way. But when the grain had sprouted and produced a crop, then the tares also appeared. So the servants of the owner came and said to him, "Sir, did you not sow good seed in your field? How then does it have tares?" He said to them, "An enemy has done this."The servants said to him, "Do you want us then to go and gather them up?' " But he said, "No, lest while you gather up the tares you also uproot the wheat with them. Let both grow together until the harvest, and at the time of harvest I will say to the reapers, "First gather together the tares and bind them in bundles to burn them, but gather the wheat into my barn." ' " —Matthew 13:24–30.

THE HARVEST TAKES PLACE AT THE END OF THE WORLD:

"The enemy who sowed them is the devil, the harvest is the end of the age, and the reapers are the angels." —Matthew 13:39.

JESUS WAITS PATIENTLY FOR THE GOOD FRUIT TO RIPEN:

"Therefore be patient, brethren, until the coming of the Lord. See how the farmer waits for the precious fruit of the earth, waiting patiently for it until it receives the early and latter rain. You also be patient. Establish your hearts, for the coming of the Lord is at hand." —James 5:7, 8.

PARABLE OF THE HARVEST AT THE SECOND COMING:

"And He said, 'The kingdom of God is as if a man should scatter seed on the ground, and should sleep by night and rise by day, and the seed should sprout and grow, he himself does not know how. For the earth yields crops by itself: first the blade, then the head, after that the full grain in the head. But when the grain ripens, immediately he puts in the sickle, because the harvest has come.' " —Mark 4:26–29.

CHAPTER 22

THE GLORIOUS RETURN OF OUR KING

To those who love and follow Jesus, His return in person to this earth is called "The Blessed Hope"! When Jesus comes, time will be replaced by eternity. Those asleep in the tombs and graves will be called to life. Christ's followers who are alive to meet Him will be reunited with the loved ones they have lost in death. The reign of Satan, sin, and selfishness will be at an end. No more wars. No more bloodshed. The saved of all history will enter eternity with perfect bodies and minds, free of injury, deformity, disease, or the signs of aging. What a glorious day!

What promises and predictions does the Bible offer concerning Christ's coming?

"Let not your heart be troubled; you believe in God, believe also in Me. In My Father's house are many mansions; if it were not so, I would have told you. I go to prepare a place for you. And if I go and prepare a place for you, I will come again and receive you to Myself; that where I am, there you may be also." —John 14:1–3.

"So Christ was offered once to bear the sins of many. To those who eagerly wait for Him He will appear a second time, apart from sin, for salvation." —Hebrews 9:28.

"I Will Come Again!"

Do we know when Jesus is coming again?

WE DON'T KNOW THE EXACT DAY OR HOUR:

"But of that day and hour no one knows, not even the angels of heaven, but My Father only." —Matthew 24:36.

IMMEDIATELY AFTER ALL THE SIGNS HAVE BEEN FULFILLED:

"Then the sign of the Son of Man will appear in heaven, and then all the tribes of the earth will mourn, and they will see the Son of Man coming on the clouds of heaven with power and great glory. And He will send His angels with a great sound of a trumpet, and they will gather together His elect from the four winds, from one end of heaven to the other. Now learn this parable from the fig tree: When its branch has already become tender and puts forth leaves, you know that summer is near. So you also, when you see all these things, know that it is near—at the doors!" —Matthew 24:30–33.

AFTER THE GOSPEL HAS BEEN PREACHED TO ALL THE WORLD:

"And this gospel of the kingdom will be preached in all the world as a witness to all the nations, and then the end will come." —Matthew 24:14.

How will Jesus return?

IN THE SAME WAY HE ASCENDED:

"Now when He had spoken these things, while they watched, He was taken up, and a cloud received Him out of their sight. And while they looked steadfastly toward heaven as He went up, behold, two men stood by them in white apparel, who also said, 'Men of Galilee, why do you stand gazing up into heaven? This same Jesus, who was taken up from you into heaven, will so come in like manner as you saw Him go into heaven.'" —Acts 1:9–11.

EVERY EYE WILL SEE HIM:

"Behold, He is coming with clouds, and every eye will see Him, even they who pierced Him. And all the tribes of the earth will mourn because of Him. Even so, Amen." —Revelation 1:7.

HE WILL NOT COME SILENTLY:

"Our God shall come, and shall not keep silent; a fire shall devour before Him, and it shall be very tempestuous all around Him." —Psalm 50:3.

What will Jesus do when He comes?

REWARD EVERYONE ACCORDING TO HIS WORKS:

"For the Son of Man will come in the glory of His Father with His angels, and then He will reward each according to his works." —Matthew 16:27.

GIVE EACH SAINT A CROWN OF RIGHTEOUSNESS:

"For I am already being poured out as a drink offering, and the time of my departure is at hand. I have fought the good fight, I have finished the race, I have kept the faith. Finally, there is laid up for me the crown of righteousness, which the Lord, the righteous Judge, will give to me on that Day, and not to me only but also to all who have loved His appearing." —2 Timothy 4:6–8.

How should we prepare to meet Jesus at His coming?

WATCH AND BE READY:

"Watch therefore, for you do not know what hour your Lord is coming. But know this, that if the master of the house had known what hour the thief would come, he would have watched and not allowed his house to be broken into. Therefore you also be ready, for the Son of Man is coming at an hour you do not expect." —Matthew 24:42–44.

LIVE SOBERLY, RIGHTEOUSLY, AND GODLY:

"For the grace of God that brings salvation has appeared to all men, teaching us that, denying ungodliness and worldly lusts, we should live soberly, righteously, and godly in the present age, looking for the blessed hope and glorious appearing of our great God and Savior Jesus Christ." —Titus 2:11–13.

BE PATIENT:

"Therefore be patient, brethren, until the coming of the Lord. See how the farmer waits for the precious fruit of the earth, waiting patiently for it until it receives the early and latter rain. You also be patient. Establish your hearts, for the coming of the Lord is at hand." —James 5:7, 8.

ABIDE IN HIM:

"And now, little children, abide in Him, that when He appears, we may have confidence and not be ashamed before Him at His coming." —1 John 2:28.

Lift up the trumpet, and loud let it ring:
Jesus is coming again!
Cheer up, ye pilgrims, be joyful and sing:
Jesus is coming again!
[Refrain ...]
Coming again, coming again,
Jesus is coming again!
Echo it, hilltops; proclaim it, ye plains:
Jesus is coming again!
Coming in glory, the Lamb that was slain;
Jesus is coming again!
Refrain
Heavings of earth, tell the vast, wondering throng:
Jesus is coming again!
Tempests and whirlwinds, the anthem prolong;
Jesus is coming again!
Refrain
Nations are angry—by this we do know
Jesus is coming again!
Knowledge increases; men run to and fro;
Jesus is coming again!
Refrain

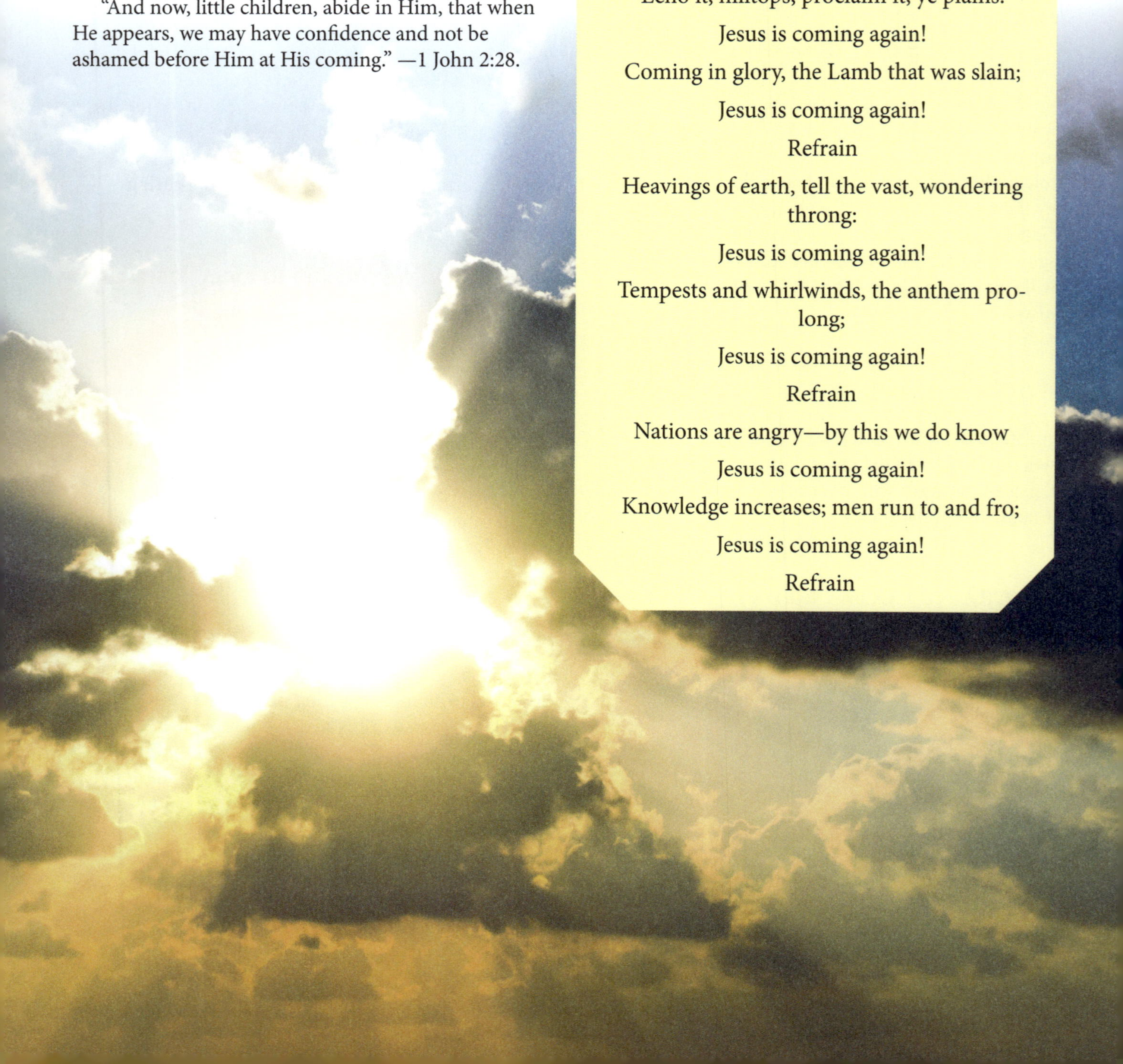

Image by Remnant Publications.

CHAPTER 23

Image by Remnant Publications.

The word millennium is not found in the Bible. It comes from the Latin word *mille*, meaning one thousand—and the Latin word *annus*, meaning year. But the Bible does indeed speak of a period of one thousand years that begins with Christ's Second Coming to earth—and His lesser-known Third Coming to earth again after a thousand years in heaven with His saved and faithful followers. It is important to discover the events that take place at the beginning of the millennium, those that happen during the millennium, and those at the close of the thousand years.

What does the Bible tell us takes place at the beginning of the millennium?

DEAD IN CHRIST RESURRECTED; LIVING RIGHTEOUS CAUGHT UP TO MEET THEM IN THE AIR:

"For this we say to you by the word of the Lord, that we who are alive and remain until the coming of the Lord will by no means precede those who are asleep. For the Lord Himself will descend from heaven with a shout, with the voice of an archangel, and with the trumpet of God. And the dead in Christ will rise first. Then we who are alive and remain shall be caught up together with them in the clouds to meet the Lord in the air. And thus we shall always be with the Lord. Therefore comfort one another with these words." —1 Thessalonians 4:15–18.

RIGHTEOUS DEAD RESURRECTED; RIGHTEOUS LIVING CHANGED:

"Behold, I tell you a mystery: We shall not all sleep, but we shall all be changed—in a moment, in the twinkling of an eye, at the last trumpet. For the trumpet will sound, and the dead will be raised incorruptible, and we shall be changed." —1 Corinthians 15:51, 52.

WICKED LIVING ARE DESTROYED:

"And to give you who are troubled rest with us when the Lord Jesus is revealed from heaven with His mighty angels, in flaming fire taking vengeance on those who do not know God, and on those who do not obey the gospel of our Lord Jesus Christ." —2 Thessalonians 1:7, 8.

LAWLESS WILL BE DESTROYED BY BRIGHTNESS OF CHRIST'S COMING:

"And then the lawless one will be revealed, whom the Lord will consume with the breath of His mouth and destroy with the brightness of His coming." —2 Thessalonians 2:8.

SATAN BOUND TO DESOLATE EARTH FOR A THOUSAND YEARS:

"Then I saw an angel coming down from heaven, having the key to the bottomless pit and a great chain in his hand. He laid hold of the dragon, that serpent of old, who is the Devil and Satan, and bound him for a thousand years; and he cast him into the bottomless pit, and shut him up, and set a seal on him, so that he should deceive the nations no more till the thousand years were finished. But after these things he must be released for a little while." —Revelation 20:1–3.

What does the Bible tell us takes place during the millennium?

RIGHTEOUS WILL BE IN HEAVEN JUDGING WICKED:

"Dare any of you, having a matter against another, go to law before the unrighteous, and not before the saints? Do you not know that the saints will judge the world? And if the world will be judged by you, are you unworthy to judge the smallest matters? Do you not know that we shall judge angels? How much more, things that pertain to this life?" —1 Corinthians 6:1–3.

What does the Bible tell us takes place at the end of the millennium?

WICKED DEAD ARE RAISED:

"But the rest of the dead did not live again until the thousand years were finished. This is the first resurrection."—Revelation 20:5.

SATAN IS LOOSED:

"Now when the thousand years have expired, Satan will be released from his prison and will go out to deceive the nations which are in the four corners of the earth, Gog and Magog, to gather them together to battle, whose number is as the sand of the sea." —Revelation 20:7, 8.

HOLY CITY DESCENDS FROM HEAVEN:

"Then I, John, saw the holy city, New Jerusalem, coming down out of heaven from God, prepared as a bride adorned for her husband." —Revelation 21:2.

SATAN AND THE WICKED SURROUND THE CITY; FIRE DESTROYS THEM:

"They went up on the breadth of the earth and surrounded the camp of the saints and the beloved city. And fire came down from God out of heaven and devoured them. The devil, who deceived them, was cast into the lake of fire and brimstone where the beast and the false prophet are. And they will be tormented day and night forever and ever." —Revelation 20:9, 10.

FIRE PURIFIES THE EARTH, AND GOD MAKES IT ANEW:

"But the day of the Lord will come as a thief in the night, in which the heavens will pass away with a great noise, and the elements will melt with fervent heat; both the earth and the works that are in it will be burned up. Therefore, since all these things will be dissolved, what manner of persons ought you to be in holy conduct and godliness, looking for and hastening the coming of the day of God, because of which the heavens will be dissolved, being on fire, and the elements will melt with fervent heat? Nevertheless we, according to His promise, look for new heavens and a new earth in which righteousness dwells." —2 Peter 3:10–13.

Image by Remnant Publications

CHAPTER 24

HEAVEN—OUR ETERNAL HOME

Once Jesus returns, everything changes! For a thousand years, Christ's followers live in heaven, with immortal, youthful, perfect bodies and minds. Peace reigns. Conflict is gone. Temptation, stress, pain, death, and tears no longer plague us. Then, at the end of the millennium, God descends with the Holy City, New Jerusalem, to this earth, with all of His followers. Satan and the resurrected wicked make one last effort for control of the city and the universe, then they perish. From then on, we live in a sin-free, perfect universe where love rules!

Can we even now look forward to new heavens and a new earth?

"Nevertheless we, according to His promise, look for new heavens and a new earth in which righteousness dwells." —2 Peter 3:13.

THE PROPHET ISAIAH DESCRIBES OUR NEW HOME:

"Say to those who are fearful-hearted, 'Be strong, do not fear! Behold, your God will come with vengeance, with the recompense of God; He will come and save you.' Then the eyes of the blind shall be opened, and the ears of the deaf shall be unstopped. Then the lame shall leap like a deer, and the tongue of the dumb sing. For waters shall burst forth in the wilderness, and streams in the desert. The parched ground shall become a pool, and the thirsty land springs of water; in the habitation of jackals, where each lay, there shall be grass with reeds and rushes. A highway shall be there, and a road, and it shall be called the Highway of Holiness. The unclean shall not pass over it, but it shall be for others. Whoever walks the road, although a fool, shall not go astray. No lion shall be there, nor shall any ravenous beast go up on it; it shall not be found there. But the redeemed shall walk there, and the ransomed of the Lord shall return, and come to Zion with singing, with everlasting joy on their heads. They shall obtain joy and gladness, and sorrow and sighing shall flee away." —Isaiah 35:4–10.

ISAIAH CONTINUES HIS DESCRIPTION OF OUR ETERNAL HOME:

" 'For behold, I create new heavens and a new earth; and the former shall not be remembered or come to mind. But be glad and rejoice forever in what I create; for behold, I create Jerusalem as a rejoicing, and her people a joy. I will rejoice in Jerusalem, and joy in My people; the voice of weeping shall no longer be heard in her, nor the voice of crying. No more shall an infant from there live but a few days, nor an old man who has not fulfilled his days; for the child shall die one hundred years old, but the sinner being one hundred years old shall be accursed. They shall build houses and inhabit them; they shall plant vineyards and eat their fruit. They shall not build and another inhabit; they shall not plant and another eat; for as the days of a tree, so shall be the days of My people, and My elect shall long enjoy the work of their hands. They shall not labor in vain, nor bring forth children for trouble; for they shall be the descendants of the blessed of the Lord, and their offspring with them. It shall come to pass that before they call, I will answer; and while they are still speaking, I will hear. The wolf and the lamb shall feed together, the lion shall eat straw like the ox, and dust shall be the serpent's food. They shall not hurt nor destroy in all My holy mountain,' says the Lord." —Isaiah 65:17–25.

The apostle John also describes our eternal home

"Now I saw a new heaven and a new earth, for the first heaven and the first earth had passed away. Also there was no more sea. Then I, John, saw the holy city, New Jerusalem, coming down out of heaven from God, prepared as a bride adorned for her husband. And I heard a loud voice from heaven saying, 'Behold, the tabernacle of God is with men, and He will dwell with them, and they shall be His people. God Himself will be with them and be their God. And God will wipe away every tear from their eyes; there shall be no more death, nor sorrow, nor crying. There shall be no more pain, for the former things have passed away.' Then He who sat on the throne said, 'Behold, I make all things new.' And He said to me, 'Write, for these words are true and faithful.' " —Revelation 21:1–5.

"And he showed me a pure river of water of life, clear as crystal, proceeding from the throne of God and of the Lamb. In the middle of its street, and on either side of the river, was the tree of life, which bore twelve fruits, each tree yielding its fruit every month. The leaves of the tree were for the healing of the nations. And there shall be no more curse, but the throne of God and of the Lamb shall be in it, and His servants shall serve Him. They shall see His face, and His name shall be on their foreheads. There shall be no night there: They need no lamp nor light of the sun, for the Lord God gives them light. And they shall reign forever and ever." —Revelation 22:1–5.

JOHN DESCRIBES THE HOLY CITY, NEW JERUSALEM:

"And he carried me away in the Spirit to a great and high mountain, and showed me the great city, the holy Jerusalem, descending out of heaven from God, having the glory of God. Her light was like a most precious stone, like a jasper stone, clear as crystal. Also she had a great and high wall with twelve gates, and twelve angels at the gates, and names written on them, which are the names of the twelve tribes of the children of Israel: three gates on the east, three gates on the north, three gates on the south, and three gates on the west. Now the wall of the city had twelve foundations, and on them were the names of the twelve apostles of the Lamb. And he who talked with me had a gold reed to measure the city, its gates, and its wall. The city is laid out as a square; its length is as great as its breadth. And he measured the city with the reed: twelve thousand furlongs. Its length, breadth, and height are equal. Then he measured its wall: one hundred and forty-four cubits, according to the measure of a man, that is, of an angel. The construction of its wall was of jasper; and the city was pure gold, like clear glass. The foundations of the wall of the city were adorned with all kinds of precious stones: the first foundation was jasper, the second sapphire, the third chalcedony, the fourth emerald, the fifth sardonyx, the sixth sardius, the seventh chrysolite, the eighth beryl, the ninth topaz, the tenth chrysoprase, the eleventh jacinth, and the twelfth amethyst. The twelve gates were twelve pearls: each individual gate was of one pearl. And the street of

the city was pure gold, like transparent glass. But I saw no temple in it, for the Lord God Almighty and the Lamb are its temple. The city had no need of the sun or of the moon to shine in it, for the glory of God illuminated it. The Lamb is its light. And the nations of those who are saved shall walk in its light, and the kings of the earth bring their glory and honor into it. Its gates shall not be shut at all by day (there shall be no night there). And they shall bring the glory and the honor of the nations into it." —Revelation 21:10–26.

OUR ONLY RESPONSE TO THE PROSPECT OF FINALLY BEING HOME:

"He who testifies to these things says, 'Surely I am coming quickly.' Amen. Even so, come, Lord Jesus!" —Revelation 22:20.

NOTES

ooks You Can Trust!

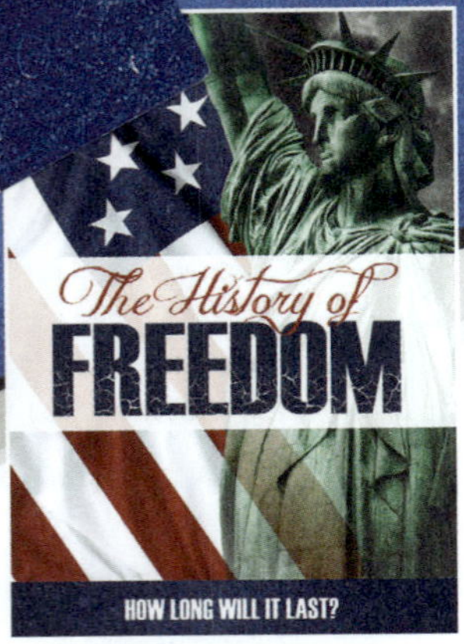

The History of Freedom

Are you ready to dig deeper into God's word? Are you ready to discover for yourself the truth about the last days?

Your Questions God's Answers

God's answers from the Bible. Is there hope? What will be the signs of the end of the world, and many others.

In Search of Peace

An all time best-seller, printed in over 100 languages. Find the answer to problems people are facing like how to achieve freedom from worry, guilt, and fear.

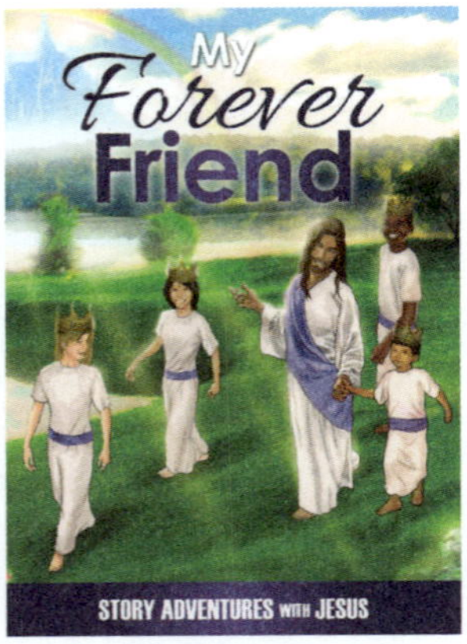

My Forever Friend

Each story from the life of Christ features beautiful artwork and suggested activities that parents and children can do together.

Real Heroes
Amazing Stories from the Bible

The Bible is full of great stories. Your children will love to read about the faith and courage of God's followers.

Storytime
Character-building Stories for Children

As your children read this book, thoughtful questions will help them reflect on important lessons and apply them to their own lives.

Give Them Something Better

Beautiful, Delicious, Nutritious, Fresh. That is what every meal should be and can be with this wonderful new resource.

Live Life to the Fullest

Learn to Live – the 8 Essentials of Optimum Health. Choice, rest, environment, activity, trust, interpersonal relationships, outlook and nutrition.

Habits that Heal: Habits from America's Longest Living People

A group of people in Loma Linda, California, are known as one of the world's healthiest longest living people. Discover the secret to their long, healthy lives.

FAMILY HOME CHRISTIAN BOOKS

To order visit: www.FamilyHomeChristianBooks.com
or call now: (800) 4-A-NEW-LIFE (800) 426-3954